Elements of
Language
**Introductory
Course**

ASSESSMENT

Assessment Alternatives

Holistic Scoring: Prompts and Models

Rubrics for
- writing assignments
- optional projects
- oral and visual literacy
  projects and performances

Portfolio Management

Inventory Forms

Evaluation Forms

HOLT, RINEHART AND WINSTON

A Harcourt Classroom Education Company

Austin · New York · Orlando · Atlanta · San Francisco · Boston · Dallas · Toronto · London

STAFF CREDITS

EDITORIAL

Director
Mescal Evler

Manager of Editorial Operations
Bill Wahlgren

Executive Editor
Emily Shenk

Project Editor
Megan Truex

Prototyping Editor
Cheryl Christian

Contributing Editors
Jane Archer Feinstein, Ann
Michelle Gibson, Sean W. Henry,
Errol Smith, Tressa Sanders

Copyediting
Michael Neibergall, *Copyediting
Manager;* Mary Malone, *Senior
Copyeditor;* Joel Bourgeois,
Elizabeth Dickson, Gabrielle
Field, Jane Kominek, Millicent
Ondras, Theresa Reding,

Kathleen Scheiner, Laurie
Schlesinger, *Copyeditors*

Project Administration
Marie Price, *Managing Editor;*
Lori De La Garza, *Editorial
Operations Coordinator;*
Thomas Browne, Heather
Cheyne, Diane Hardin, Mark
Holland, Marcus Johnson, Jill
O'Neal, Joyce Rector, Janet Riley,
Kelly Tankersley, *Project
Administration;* Gail Coupland,
Ruth Hooker, Margaret Sanchez,
Word Processing

Editorial Permissions
Janet Harrington, *Permissions
Editor*

**Writers of Exemplary Student
Essays**
Zachary McCullough, Maeghan
Gibson

ART, DESIGN AND PHOTO

Graphic Services
Kristen Darby, *Manager*

Image Acquisitions
Joe London, *Director;* Tim Taylor,
Photo Research Supervisor;
Rick Benavides, *Assistant Photo
Researcher;* Elaine Tate,
Supervisor; Erin Cone, *Art Buyer*

Cover Design
Sunday Patterson

PRODUCTION

Belinda Barbosa Lopez, *Senior
Production Coordinator*
Simira Davis, *Supervisor*
Nancy Hargis, *Media Production
Supervisor*
Joan Lindsay, *Production
Coordinator*
Beth Prevelige, *Prepress Manager*

MANUFACTURING

Michael Roche, *Supervisor of
Inventory and Manufacturing*

Dr. Roger Farr, author of the essay that appears on pages 1–23, is currently Chancellor's Professor of Education and Director of the Center for Innovation and Assessment at Indiana University. He is a past president of the International Reading Association and the author of both norm-referenced tests and performance assessments. Dr. Farr has taught at both elementary and high school levels in New York State and has served as a school district reading consultant.

The International Reading Association presented Dr. Farr the William S. Gray award for outstanding lifetime contributions to the teaching of reading in 1984. He was elected to the IRA for outstanding lifetime contributions to the teaching of reading in 1984. He was elected to the IRA Reading Hall of Fame in 1986 and was selected by the IRA as the Outstanding Teacher Educator in Reading in 1988.

Printed in the United States of America

ISBN 0-03-057566-4

12345 179 04 03 02 01 00

Table of Contents

Portfolio Management

Forms for evaluating and organizing portfolio work

Forms for communication with parents and guardians and for assessing student language use

Inventories and Evaluation Forms

Peer and self-assessment forms for recording student reading, establishing baselines, and setting goals

Table of Contents

Forms for tracking student improvement in reading

Writing Forms

Peer and self-assessment forms for recording student writing, establishing baselines, and setting goals

Table of Contents

Forms for tracking student improvement in writing

Peer and self-assessment forms for recording student speaking and listening activities, establishing baselines, and setting goals

Forms for tracking student improvement in speaking and listening

Table of Contents

Table of Contents

Writing Assessment

Evaluation Rubrics

About This Book

This booklet, *Assessment Alternatives,* accompanies the *Elements of Language* series and provides assessment resources for portfolio work, essays written in testing situations, and a variety of classroom activities.

Part I

Portfolio Management

This section begins with an essay designed to provide an introduction to portfolio work, including suggestions about how to develop and use portfolios and how to conduct conferences with students about their work.

The introductory essay is followed by a set of student forms for assessing and organizing portfolio contents and for setting goals for future work. Also included is a set of teacher forms for communicating with parents or guardians about student work and for generally assessing students' progress.

Part II

Inventories and Evaluation Forms

These forms can be used to record work, to establish baselines and goals, and to think critically about student work in a variety of areas. These areas include:

- **Reading**
- **Writing**
- **Speaking and Listening**
- **Viewing and Representing**
- **Cooperative Learning**

The goal of these forms is to encourage students to develop criteria for assessing their work and to identify areas for improvement. Many forms can also be used for assessment of a peer's work.

A set of forms for the teacher to use in assessing student progress can be found after the set of student forms for each content area.

Part III

Writing Assessment

This section contains three different kinds of rubrics for assessing on-demand writing: *Six Point Scales, Four Point Scales,* and *Six Trait Scales.* Accompanying these scales are high-level, mid-level, and low-level examples of student writing. Individual evaluations, based on each of the three rubrics, follow each student essay.

Part IV

Evaluation Rubrics

Included in this section are sets of criteria for evaluating all *Focus On* workshops and *Choices* activities included in the pupil's edition. These rubrics may be used by students for peer or self-assessment or by the teacher for assessing student work.

Portfolio Assessment in the Language Arts

Although establishing and using a portfolio assessment system requires a certain amount of time, effort, and understanding, an increasing number of teachers believe that the benefits of implementing such a system richly reward their efforts.

Language arts portfolios are collections of materials that display aspects of students' use of language. They are a means by which students can collect samples of their written work over time so that they and their teachers can ascertain how the students are developing as language users. Because reflection and self-assessment are built-in aspects of language arts portfolios, both also help students develop their critical-thinking and metacognitive abilities.

Each portfolio collection is typically kept in a folder, box, or other container to which items are added on a regular basis. The collection can include a great variety of materials, depending on the design of the portfolio assessment program, the kinds of projects completed inside and outside of the classroom, and the interests of individual students. For example, portfolios may contain student stories, essays, sketches, poems, letters, journals, and other original writing, and they may also contain reactions to articles, stories, and other texts the student has read. Other materials that are suitable for inclusion in portfolios are drawings, photographs, audiotapes, and videotapes of students taking part in special activities; clippings and pictures from newspapers and magazines; and notes on favorite authors and on stories and books that the student hopes to read. Many portfolios also include several versions of the same piece of writing, demonstrating how the writing has developed through revision.

Finally, portfolios may contain logs of things the student has read or written, written reflections or assessments of portfolio work, and tables and explanations about the way the portfolio is organized. (A collection of forms that can be used to generate these items may be found on page 24 following this essay and in Part II of this booklet.)

The Advantages of Portfolio Assessment

How can portfolio assessment help you meet your instructional goals? Here are some of the most important advantages of using portfolios:

- *Portfolios link instruction and assessment.* Traditional testing is usually one or more steps removed from the process or performance being assessed. However, because portfolio assessment focuses on performance—on students' actual use of language—portfolios are a highly accurate gauge of what students have learned in the classroom.

- *Portfolios involve students in assessing their own language use and abilities.* Portfolio assessment can provide some of the most effective learning opportunities available in your classroom. In fact, the assessment is itself instructional: Students, as self-assessors, identify their own strengths and weaknesses. Furthermore, portfolios are a natural way to develop metacognition in your students. As the collected work is analyzed, the student begins to think critically about how he or she makes meaning while reading, writing, speaking, and listening. For example, the student begins to ask questions while reading, such as "Is this telling me what I need to know?" "Am I enjoying this author as much as I expected to?" "Why or why not?" While writing, the student may ask, "Am I thinking about the goals I set when I was analyzing my portfolio?" That's what good instruction is all about: getting students to use the skills you help them develop.

- *Portfolios invite attention to important aspects of language.* Because most portfolios include numerous writing samples, they naturally direct attention to diction, style, main idea or theme, author's purpose, and other aspects of language that are difficult to assess in other ways. The portfolio encourages awareness and appreciation of these aspects of language as they occur in literature and nonfiction as well as in the student's own work.

- *Portfolios emphasize language use as a process that integrates language behaviors.* Students who keep and analyze portfolios develop an understanding that reading, writing, speaking, listening, viewing, and representing are all aspects of a larger process. They come to see that language behaviors are connected by thinking about and expressing one's own ideas and feelings.

- *Portfolios make students aware of audience and the need for a writing purpose.* Students develop audience awareness by regularly analyzing their portfolio writing samples. Evaluation forms prompt them to reflect on whether they have defined and appropriately addressed their audience. Moreover, because portfolios provide or support opportunities for students to work together, peers can often provide feedback about how well a student has addressed an audience in his or her work. Finally, students may be asked to consider particular audiences (parents, classmates, or community groups, for example) who will review their portfolios; they may prepare explanations of the contents for such audiences, and they may select specific papers to present as a special collection to such audiences.

- *Portfolios provide a vehicle for student interaction and cooperative learning.* Many projects that normally involve cooperative learning produce material for portfolios. Portfolios, in turn, provide or support many opportunities for students to work together. Students

As they become attuned to audience, students automatically begin to be more focused on whether their work has fulfilled their purpose for writing. They begin to ask:"Did I say what I meant to say? Could I have been clearer and more effective? Do I understand what this writer wants to tell me? Do I agree with it?" Speaking and listening activities can also be evaluated in terms of audience awareness and clarity of purpose.

can work as partners or as team members who critique each other's collections. For example, students might work together to prepare, show, and explain portfolios to particular audiences, such as parents, administrators, and other groups interested in educational progress and accountability.

- ***Portfolios can incorporate many types of student expression on a variety of topics.*** Students should be encouraged to include materials from different subject areas and from outside school, especially materials related to hobbies and other special interests. In this way, students come to see language arts skills as crucial tools for authentic, real-world work.

- ***Portfolios provide genuine opportunities to learn about students and their progress as language users.*** Portfolio contents can reveal to the teacher a great deal about the student's background and interests with respect to reading, writing, speaking, listening, viewing, and representing. Portfolios can also demonstrate the student's development as a language user and reveal areas where he or she needs improvement.

How to Develop and Use Portfolios

As you begin designing a portfolio program for your students, you may wish to read articles and reports that discuss the advantages of portfolio assessment. The reading list on page 23 can help you get started.

You may want to require that certain papers, projects, and reports be included in the portfolio. Such requirements should be kept to a minimum so that students feel that they can include whatever they consider to be relevant to their language development.

Portfolios that include such planning papers and intermediate drafts are called *working portfolios*. Working portfolios force the student to organize and analyze the material collected, an activity that makes clear to the student that language use is process.

Basic Design Features

For a portfolio program to be successful in the classroom, the program should reflect the teacher's particular instructional goals and the students' needs as learners. Teachers are encouraged to customize a portfolio program for their classrooms, although most successful portfolio programs share a core of essential portfolio management techniques. Following are suggestions that teachers will want to consider in customizing a portfolio program.

- *Integrate portfolio assessment into the regular classroom routine.* Teachers should make portfolio work a regular class activity by providing opportunities for students to work with their collections during class time. During these portfolio sessions, the teacher should promote analysis (assessment) that reflects his or her instructional objectives and goals.
- *Link the program to classroom activities.* Student portfolios should contain numerous examples of classroom activities and projects. To ensure that portfolios reflect the scope of students' work, some teachers require that certain papers and assignments be included.
- *Let students have the control.* Students can develop both self-assessment and metacognition skills when they select and arrange portfolio contents themselves. This practice also develops a strong sense of ownership: students feel that their portfolios belong to them, not to the teacher. When students take ownership of their work, they accept more responsibility for their own language development. To encourage a sense of ownership on the part of students, portfolios should be stored where students can get at them easily, and students should have regular and frequent access to their portfolios.
- *Include students' creative efforts.* To ensure that the portfolios develop a range of language skills, encourage students to include samples of their creative writing, pieces they have written outside of class, and publishing activities that they may have participated in, such as the production of a class magazine.
- *Make sure portfolios record students' writing process.* If portfolios are to teach language use as a process that integrates various language behaviors, they need to contain papers that show how writing grows out of planning and develops through revision. Portfolios should include notes, outlines, clippings, reactions to reading or oral presentations, pictures, and other materials that inspired the final product. Equally vital to the

How to Develop and Use Portfolios *(continued)*

The act of selecting particular papers to show to special audiences—parents, another teacher, or the principal, to name a few—refines students' sense of audience. Preparing and presenting selected collections, called *show portfolios*, engages students in a more sophisticated analysis of their work and encourages them to visualize the audience for the show collection.

portfolio collections are the different drafts of papers that demonstrate revision over a period of time. Such collections can promote fruitful, concrete discussions between student and teacher about how the student's process shaped the final product.

- *Rely on reactions to reading and listening.* If portfolios are to link and interrelate language behaviors, students must be encouraged to include reactions to things they read and hear. During conferences, teachers may want to point out how some of the student's work has grown out of listening or reading.

- *Encourage students to consider the audience.* Portfolio building prompts students to think about the audience because, as a kind of publication, the portfolio invites a variety of readers. Students will become interested in and sensitive to the reactions of their classmates and their teacher, as well as to the impact of the collections on any other audiences that may be allowed to view them.

- *Promote collaborative products.* Portfolios can promote student collaboration if the program sets aside class time for students to react to one another's work and to work in groups. This interaction can occur informally or in more structured student partnerships or team responses. In addition, many writing projects can be done by teams and small groups, and any common product can be reproduced for all participants' portfolios. Performance projects, speeches, and other oral presentations often require cooperative participation. Audiotapes and videotapes of collaborative projects may be included in portfolios.

If students feel free to include writing and reading done outside of class in their portfolios, you can discover interests, opinions, and concerns that can be touched on during conferences. In turn, by communicating interest in and respect for what engages the student, you can promote the success of the portfolio program.

- *Let the portfolios reflect a variety of subject areas and interests.* The language arts portfolio should include material from subject areas other than language arts. Broadening the portfolio beyond the language arts classroom is important if the student is to understand that reading, writing, speaking, and listening are authentic activities—that is, that they are central to all real-world activities. Any extensive attempt to limit portfolio contents may suggest to students that reading and writing skills relate only to the language arts classroom.

Initial Design Considerations

Using what you have read so far, you can make some initial notes as guidelines for drafting your portfolio assessment design. You can complete a chart like the one on the next page to plan how you will use portfolios and what you can do to make them effective.

How to Develop and Use Portfolios *(continued)*

What are my primary goals in developing my students' ability to use language?	How can portfolios contribute to meeting these goals?	What design features can ensure this?

How to Develop and Use Portfolios *(continued)*

Some key considerations for designing a portfolio program have been suggested above. Other considerations will arise as you assess ways to use the portfolios. Here are some questions that will probably arise in the planning stages of portfolio assessment.

How can I introduce students to the concepts of portfolio management?

What examples of student work should go into the portfolios?

What should the criteria be for deciding what will be included?

How and where will the portfolio collections be kept?

Designing a Portfolio Program

How can I introduce students to the concepts of portfolio management?

One way is to experiment with a group of your students. If you use this limited approach, be sure to select students with varied reading and writing abilities to get a sense of how portfolios work for students with a range of skill levels. To introduce portfolio assessment to them, you can either talk to students individually or as a group about what they will be doing. If other students begin expressing an interest in keeping portfolios, let them take part as well. The kind of excitement that builds around portfolio keeping almost guarantees that some students not included initially will want to get on board for the trial run; some may start keeping portfolios on their own.

You might let students help you design or at least plan some details of the system. After explaining both the reasons for keeping portfolios and the elements of the program that you have decided are essential, you can let students discuss how they think certain aspects should be handled. Even if you decide you want students to make important decisions concerning the program's design, you will need to have a clear idea of what your teaching objectives are and of what you will ask students to do.

What examples of student work should go into the portfolios?

Portfolios should reflect as much as possible the spectrum of your students' language use. What you want to ensure is that student self-assessment leads to the understanding that language skills are essential to all learning. For this to happen, portfolios should contain reading, writing, speaking, listening, viewing, and representing activities that relate to a number of subject areas and interests, not just to the language arts. Moreover, the portfolio should include final, completed works as well as drafts, notes, freewriting, and other samples that show the student's thinking and writing process.

FINAL PRODUCTS Students should consider including pieces that are created with a general audience in mind; writing that is communicative and intended for particular audiences; and writing that is very personal and that is used as a method of thinking through situations, evaluating experiences, or musing simply for enjoyment. The portfolios can contain a variety of finished products, including

- original stories, dialogue, and scripts
- poems

How to Develop and Use Portfolios *(continued)*

- essays, themes, sketches
- song lyrics
- original videos
- video or audio recordings of performances
- narrative accounts of experiences
- correspondence with family members and friends
- stream-of-consciousness pieces
- journals of various types

Examples of various types of journals that students might enjoy keeping are described below.

Keeping Journals

A journal is an excellent addition to a portfolio—and one that teachers report is very successful. Journal keeping develops the habit of recording one's observations, feelings, and ideas. At the same time, journal writing is an excellent way to develop fluency. Specifically, it can help tentative writers to overcome the reluctance to put thoughts down as words. Journal keeping can be a bridge over inhibitions to writing and can become a student's favorite example of his or her language use. All this recommends the addition of journals to the portfolio.

The success with journals in encouraging young writers has led teachers to experiment with a variety of types:

PERSONAL JOURNAL This form of journal allows the writer to make frequent entries (regularly or somewhat irregularly) on any topic and for any purpose. This popular and satisfying kind of journal writing develops writing fluency and reveals to students the essential relationship between thinking and writing. (If the journal is kept in the portfolio, you may wish to remind students that you will be viewing it. Tell students to omit anything they would not be comfortable sharing.)

LITERARY JOURNAL OR READER'S LOG This journal provides a way of promoting open-ended and freewheeling responses to student reading. Students are usually allowed to structure and organize these journals in any way that satisfies them. As a collection of written responses, the literary journal is a valuable source of notes for oral and written expression; it can also give students ideas for further reading. Finally, the literary journal is another tool that reveals to students that reading, writing, and thinking are interrelated.

TOPICAL JOURNAL This style of journal is dedicated to a particular interest or topic. It is a valuable experience for students to be allowed to express themselves freely about a specific topic—a favorite hobby, pastime, or issue, for example.

How to Develop and Use Portfolios *(continued)*

As with the literary journal, the topical journal can point students toward project ideas and further reading.

DIALOGUE JOURNAL For this journal format, students select one person—a classmate, friend, family member, or teacher, for example—to strike up a continuing dialogue with. Dialogue journals help develop audience awareness and can promote cooperative learning. If students in your class are keeping dialogue journals with each other, be prepared to help them decide in whose portfolio the journal will go. (Because making copies may be too time consuming or expensive, you could help students arrange alternate custody, or have them experiment by keeping two distinct journals.)

Fragments and Works in Progress

In addition to finished products, portfolios should include papers showing how your students are processing ideas as readers, writers, speakers, and listeners. Drafts that show how writing ideas are developed through revision are especially helpful as students assess their work. Items that demonstrate how your language users are working with their collections can include

- articles, news briefs, sketches, or other sources collected and used as the basis for written or oral projects. These "seeds" may include pictures created or collected by students and used for inspiration for the subject. The portfolio may also include some items that have not yet been developed.
- reading-response notes that have figured in the planning of a paper and have been incorporated into the final work. Once again, some notes may be intended for future projects.
- other notes, outlines, or evidence of planning for papers written or ready to be drafted
- pieces in which the student is thinking out a problem or considering a topic of interest or behavior or is planning something for the future. These pieces may include pro and con arguments, and persuasive points and reactions to reading.
- freewriting, done either at school or at home
- early versions (drafts) of the latest revision of a piece of writing
- notes analyzing the student's latest draft, which may direct subsequent revision
- solicited reactions from classmates or the teacher
- a published piece accompanied by revised manuscripts showing edits

How to Develop and Use Portfolios (continued)

- correspondence from relatives and friends to which students have written a response or to which students need to respond
- journal or diary entries that are equivalent to preliminary notes or drafts of a piece of writing
- tapes of conversations or interviews to which a piece of writing refers or on which it is based

Discourage the inclusion of workbook sheets, unless they contain ideas for future student writing; they tend to obscure the message that language development is a process, a major component of which is the expression of student ideas and opinions.

While test results in general do not make good contents for portfolios, performance assessments can provide a focused example of both language processing and integration of reading and writing skills. Such performance tests are now frequently structured as realistic tasks that require reading, synthesizing, and reacting to particular texts. More often than not, these assessments guide the student through planning stages and a preliminary draft. (These parts of the assessment are rarely rated, but they lend themselves directly to self-analysis and should definitely be included with the final draft.)

What should the criteria be for deciding what will be included?

You might want to brainstorm a list of things that could be kept in your students' portfolios and then prioritize the items on your list according to which ones you think will be essential for students' development.

Teachers often want to ensure that students keep certain kinds of papers in the portfolios, while also affirming students' need for a genuine sense of ownership of their collections. Achieving a balance between these two general objectives may not be as difficult as it seems. Students can be informed at the time that they are introduced to the portfolio concept that they will be asked to keep certain items as one part of the overall project. Almost certainly, it will be necessary to explain at some point that the collections are to be working portfolios and that certain records—including many of the forms provided in this booklet—will also need to be included. As they become accustomed to analyzing the papers in their portfolios, students can be encouraged or required to select the contents of their portfolios, using criteria that they develop themselves. Teachers can help students articulate these criteria in informal and formal conferences. Following are criteria teachers or students might consider:

- papers that students think are well done and that therefore represent their best efforts, or papers that were difficult to complete
- subjects that students enjoyed writing about, or texts they have enjoyed reading; things that they think are interesting or will interest others
- things that relate to reading or writing students intend to do in the future, including ideas that may be developed into persuasive essays, details to support positions on issues, and reaction to favorite literary texts

How to Develop and Use Portfolios *(continued)*

- papers that contain ideas or procedures that students wish to remember
- incomplete essays or projects that presented some problem for the student. He or she may plan to ask a parent, teacher, or fellow student to react to the work or to earlier drafts.
- work that students would like particular viewers of the portfolio (the teacher, their parents, their classmates, and so on) to see, for some reason. This criterion is one that will dictate selections for a show portfolio; it may also determine some of the papers selected for the overall collection.

After building their collections for some time, students should be able to examine them and make lists of their selection criteria in their own words. Doing so should balance out any requirements the teacher has set for inclusion and should ensure students' sense of ownership.

A final note on selection criteria for student portfolios: While portfolios should certainly contain students' best efforts, too often teachers and students elect to collect only their "best stuff." An overemphasis on possible audiences that might view the collection can make it seem important that the collection be a show portfolio. Preparing show portfolios for particular audiences can require students to assess their work in order to decide what is worth including. That is a worthwhile experience, but once the preparation for the show has been completed, student self-assessment ends.

How and where will the portfolio collections be kept?

Part of the fun of keeping portfolios is deciding what the holders for the collections will look like. In a few classrooms, portfolio holders are standardized, but in most classes, the students are allowed to create their own. Many teachers allow students to furnish their own containers or folders, as long as these are big enough to hold the collections without students' having to fold or roll the papers—and not so large as to create storage problems. In addition, many teachers encourage their students to decorate their portfolio holders in unique, colorful, personal, and whimsical ways. Allowing this individuality creates enthusiasm for the project. It also helps students develop a genuine sense of ownership, an important attitude to foster if this system is to succeed.

The kinds of holders that students are likely to bring to school include household cardboard boxes, stationery boxes, folders of various types, paper or plastic shopping bags, computer paper boxes, and plastic and cardboard containers for storing clothing and other items. It would be a good idea to

Start collecting some samples of holders you can show when you introduce portfolio management to your students. Decorate at least one sample, or have a young friend or relative do it. At the same time, be thinking about areas in your classroom where the collections can be kept.

How to Develop and Use Portfolios *(continued)*

have several different examples to show students when discussing how they will keep their papers. It is also a good idea to have some holders on hand for students who are unable to find anything at home that they think is suitable, and for use as replacements for unworkable holders some students may bring, such as shoe boxes that are too small to hold the portfolio items.

The resulting storage area will probably not be neatly uniform but will not necessarily be unattractive, either. Teachers who want a tidier storage area might find similar boxes to pass out to all students, who are then allowed to personalize them in different ways.

The amount of space available in a particular classroom will, of course, determine where students keep their collections, but it is vital that the area be accessible to students. It will save a great deal of inconvenience during the school year if the portfolios are on open shelves or on an accessible ledge of some kind and are not too far from students. If students can retrieve and put away their portfolios in less than a minute or two, there will be many instances when portfolio work can be allowed. Deciding where to keep the portfolios is a decision that may be put off until students know enough about the process to help make the decision.

Open access to portfolios does create the possibility of students looking at classmates' collections without permission and without warning. It seems only fair to remind students not to include in their portfolio anything they would not want others to see. A caution from the teacher could save a student from a wounding embarrassment.

Conferencing with Students

If you are new at conducting portfolio conferences, ask a student who has kept one or more papers to sit down and talk with you. Talk with the student about what he or she thinks is strong about the paper, how it came to be written, and what kind of reading or research the student undertook. See how well you can promote an open-ended conversation related to the topic of the paper and to language use.

You may wish to try out the Student-Teacher Conference Notes worksheet on page 33. After the conference, think about what you could do to ensure a productive portfolio conference that would be helpful and worthwhile to students.

The regular informal exchanges between teacher and student about portfolio content are obviously very important, but the more formal conferences that anchor a successful program are of equal if not greater importance. Conferences are evidence that both the teacher and the student take the portfolio collection seriously and that the usefulness of the portfolio depends on an ongoing analysis of it. By blocking out time to conduct at least four formal conferences with each student each year, the teacher demonstrates a commitment to the program and a genuine interest in each student's progress.

Conducting Portfolio Conferences

The conference should proceed as a friendly but clearly directed conversation between the student and the teacher. The focus of the conference should be on how the use of language serves the student's needs and interests. This focus translates, in the course of the conference, into helping each student reflect on why and how he or she reads and writes.

Teachers will want to discuss with students the quantity of recent reading and writing compared with that of previous time periods, the kinds of reading and writing that the student has done, and the student's purposes for reading and writing. (Build on discussions about texts and authors by recommending related reading.) Teachers will also want to discuss how the inclusions in the portfolio came to be and whether the pieces represent experiences and ideas the student has enjoyed and thinks are important. Teachers should let students know that the portfolio documents say something important about the individual student's life. In fact, a significant portion of the conference may be dedicated to learning about the student's interests. Here are a few examples of the types of statements that might elicit a helpful response:

- You seem to know a lot about deep-sea diving.
- Where did you learn all those details?
- Have you looked for books about them?
- Why don't you write something about them?

The student, too, should feel free to ask questions:

- Which pieces seem the best to the teacher and why?
- Is it always necessary to write for some audience?
- What if a writer wants an idea or thought to be vague—remain private, though written?
- How can a writer stop to use reference materials to find the right word and spell it correctly without losing the flow of expression?

Conferencing with Students *(continued)*

These examples show how the conference can provide powerful, effective opportunities to teach and to guide language development. The conference conversations between the teacher and the student should be as unique as the individual student who joins the teacher in this exchange.

Ideally, each student will look forward to the conference as a time when student and teacher pay close attention to what the student has done; how the student feels about that performance; and what the student's needs and goals are. Such conferences encourage students to accept responsibility for their own development.

The following guidelines will help the teacher make the most of portfolio conferences.

Conference Guidelines

- *Conferences should be conducted without interruption.* Plan creatively: Perhaps a volunteer assistant can manage the rest of the class during meetings. Or, assign to other students cooperative-learning activities or other work that does not disrupt your exchange with the student. It may be necessary to conduct the conference outside class time.

- *Keep the focus on the student.* Make the conference as much like an informal conversation as possible by asking questions that will emphasize student interests, attitudes toward reading and writing, favorite authors, and topics they enjoy reading about. Demonstrate that you care what the student thinks and likes. You can also show that you respect the way a student's individuality is manifested in language use.

- *Let the conversation develop naturally.* Be an active listener: Give full attention to what the student is saying. The student's contribution is likely to suggest a question or comment from you, resulting in a genuine and natural exchange. There may be opportunities to get back to questions the teacher had hoped to ask, but teachers should respect the course that the exchange takes and realize that some of their planned questions will need to be dropped. Good listening on the part of the teacher will help create successful conferences that address individual student interests and needs.

- *Be sincere but not judgmental.* Avoid evaluating or passing judgment on interests or aspects of the student's language use. On the other hand, try to avoid continually expressing approval and thereby creating a situation in which the student tries to respond in a way that will win favor: The conference will then lose its focus on the individual's language needs and development.

For many teachers, the time and planning that the conference demands constitute the most difficult aspect of portfolio assessment. Think about how you can use all the resources at your disposal, and don't forget to enlist students' help. Ask them to help you schedule meetings, and request their cooperation so that the system functions smoothly.

Questions will undoubtedly occur to you while reviewing the student's portfolio. It may be useful to have a few notes to remind you of things you would like to ask. Do not, however, approach a conference with a list that dictates the exchange with the student.

Conferencing with Students *(continued)*

Don't hesitate to use the conference as a means of getting to know the student better by learning about his or her interests, pastimes, concerns, and opinions. This can be time well spent, particularly if it demonstrates to the student that the various aspects of his or her life can be very closely connected to the use and development of language arts skills.

Shortly after the conference, the student can translate his or her notes to a worksheet like the goal-setting form on page 31, which will ask the student to elaborate on the objectives that have been established.

- *Keep the conversation open and positive.* It is fine to ask questions that direct the focus back to the collection, as long as that leads in turn to a discussion of ideas and content, the process of reading and writing, and indications of the student's strengths and progress as a language user. In general, however, teachers should ask questions that promise to open up discussion, not shut it down. Phrase questions and comments so that they invite elaboration and explanation.

- *Gear the conference toward goal setting.* Identify and come to an agreement about the goals and objectives the student will be attending to during the next time period.

- *Limit the attention devoted to usage errors.* If the student needs to focus on mechanical or grammatical problems, suggest that over the next time period the student pay particular attention to these problems when editing and revising. Do not, however, turn the session into a catalogue of language errors encountered. Keep in mind that if there are four conferences and each one tactfully encourages a focus on just one or two examples of non-standard mechanical usage, it is possible to eliminate from four to eight high-priority errors during the course of a school year.

- *Keep joint notes with the student on the conference.* To keep a focus on the most important aspects of the conference, you and the student should use the *Student-Teacher Conference Notes* form. Frequently, student and teacher will record notes based on the same observation: For example, the student might write, "I like to use a lot of verbs at the beginning of my sentences, but maybe I use too many." And the teacher might write, "Let's watch to see how often Cody frontshifts sentence elements for emphasis." The student might write, "Look for a novel about the Civil War." The teacher might note, "Find a copy of *The Killer Angels* for Cody if possible." The model for conference notes in this guide allows the two participants to make notes on the same sheet, side by side; thus, notes on the same point will roughly correspond. The teacher and the student can even write at the same time if they can position the note sheet in a way that will facilitate this.

Keep in mind that conference notes frequently serve as a reference point for an action plan that is then more fully considered on the goal-setting worksheet.

Types of Student-Teacher Conferences

In addition to the scheduled conference, there are several other types of conferences that teachers can conduct as a part of portfolio assessment:

Conferencing with Students *(continued)*

GOAL CLARIFICATION CONFERENCES If a student appears to be having trouble using the portfolio system, a goal clarification conference can be scheduled. The meeting's focus should be to help the student clarify and articulate objectives so that work on the collection is directed and productive.

It is important that this session not be perceived as being overly critical of the student. Be supportive and positive about the collection; try to generate a discussion that will lead to clear goals for the student. These objectives can be articulated on a goal-setting worksheet, which the teacher can help the student fill out.

PUBLICATION STAFF CONFERENCES Students who are publishing pieces they write may frequently meet as teams or in staff conferences to select pieces from their portfolio. They may also discuss possible revisions of manuscripts they hope to publish. Teachers may enjoy observing and even participating in these but should let students direct them as much as possible.

Other class projects and collaborative activities can generate similar student conferences that may involve portfolio collections.

INFORMAL OR ROVING CONFERENCES In these conferences, teachers consult with students about their portfolios during impromptu sessions. For example, at any time a teacher might encounter a student with an important and intriguing question, or spot confusion or a situation developing into frustration for a self-assessor. Often the situation calls for effective questioning and then good listening, just as in the regularly scheduled conferences.

Questions and Answers

The questions that follow are frequently asked by teachers who are thinking about instituting a portfolio management system.

- How can I make my students familiar and comfortable with the idea of creating portfolios?
- How often should my students work on their portfolios?
- How can I keep the portfolios from growing too bulky to manage and analyze effectively?
- Should I grade my students' portfolios?
- Who else, besides the student and me, should be allowed to see the portfolio?
- How can I protect against the possible negative effects of allowing a wide variety of persons to see students' portfolios?

How can I make my students comfortable with portfolios?

Teachers will, of course, want to begin by describing what portfolios are and what they are designed to accomplish. One way to help students visualize portfolios is to point out that some professionals keep portfolios:

- Artists usually keep portfolios to show prospective clients or employers what kind of work they can do. In a sense, an artist's studio is one big working portfolio, full of projects in various stages of completion.
- Photographers, architects, clothing designers, interior designers, and a host of other professionals keep portfolios full of samples of their work.
- Models carry portfolios of pictures showing them in a variety of styles and situations.
- Some writers keep portfolios of their work.
- People who invest their money in stocks and bonds call the collection of different investments they hold a portfolio.

Teachers can encourage students' interest by inviting to the classroom someone who can exhibit and explain a professional portfolio. Teachers might also show students an actual language arts portfolio created by a student in another class or school. Some teachers put together a portfolio of their own and use it as an example for their students.

After this or another introduction, you might share the following information with students:

- Explain what kinds of things will go into the portfolios and why. Students can choose what to include in their collections, but teachers can indicate that a few items will be required, including some records. Without introducing all the records to be used, teachers might show and explain basic forms, such as logs. If forms filled out by students are available, use them as examples.

- Stress that portfolios will be examined regularly. If the working portfolios will be available to parents or others, be sure to inform students. If you plan for others to see only show portfolios, this might be a good time to introduce this kind of portfolio.
- Show examples of holders that might be used, and explain where they will be kept. Students can be involved in making decisions about how and where portfolios will be housed.

How often should my students work on their portfolios?

The answer is "regularly and often." Teachers should schedule half-hour sessions weekly; ideally, there will be time almost every day when students can work on their collections. The Scheduling Plan on the next page shows activities that should occur regularly in your program.

How can I keep the portfolios from growing too bulky to manage and analyze effectively?

Because portfolios are intended to demonstrate students' products and processes over time, collections should be culled only when necessary. However, working portfolios can become simply too big, bulky, and clumsy to organize and analyze. If some students find their collections too unwieldy to work with, encourage them to try one of the following techniques:

- Cull older pieces except for those that stand as the best work examples. Put the removed contents into a separate holder and complete an *About My Portfolio* record. Explain on the record that the work consists of less-favored work, and have students take it home for parents to examine and/or save. Photocopies of later work that you consider more successful can be included as comparison.
- Close the whole collection, except for writing not yet completed, notes and records the student intends to use, and other idea files. Send the entire collection home with an explanation record and start a new portfolio.
- Cull from the collection one or more show portfolios for particular audiences, such as parents, other relatives, other teachers, administrators, or supervisors. After the show portfolio has been viewed, return it to the rest of the collection. Start a new portfolio, beginning with the ideas in progress.

Some teachers have their students prepare a larger decorated box to take home at the beginning of the school year. This container eventually holds banded groups of papers culled during the year. Students then have one repository for their entire portfolio collection, which they can keep indefinitely.

Questions and Answers *(continued)*

SCHEDULING PLAN FOR PORTFOLIO ASSESSMENT

Activity	Frequency	The Student	The Teacher
Keeping logs	As reading, writing, and other language experiences are completed; daily if necessary	Makes the entries on the *My Reading Record, My Writing Record, My Speaking and Listening Record,* and My *Viewing Record*	Encourages the student to make regular entries and discusses with the student indications of progress, developing interests, etc.
Collecting writing samples, reactions to reading, entries that reflect on oral language	As drafts and reactions to reading become available; can be as often as daily	Selects materials to be included	Can select materials to be included; may require some inclusions
Keeping journal(s)	Ongoing basis; daily to at least once a week	Makes regular entries in one or more journals	Analyzes journal writing discreetly and confidentially
Adding notes, pictures, clippings, and other idea sources	Weekly or more often	Clips and collects ideas and adds them to appropriate place in the portfolio	Reacts to student's idea sources (every month or so); discusses with student how he or she will use them
Explaining, analyzing, evaluating inclusions	Weekly; not less than every other week	Uses forms for evaluating and organizing work to analyze and describe individual pieces included	Analyzes inclusions and student analysis of them at least four times a year—before conferences
Completing summary analyses	Monthly and always before conference	Completes a *Summary of Progress* record while comparing it with previously completed summary	Completes selected *Progress Reports* at least four times a year—before conferences, relying on student summaries and previously completed records
Conferencing—informal	Ongoing; ideally, at least once a week	Freely asks teacher for advice as often as needed; shares emerging observations with teacher	Makes an effort to observe student working on portfolio at least every two weeks and to discuss one or more specific new inclusions and analyses
Conferencing—formal	At least four times a year	Prepares for conference by completing summaries; discusses portfolio contents and analysis of them with teacher; devises new goals; takes joint notes	Prepares for conference with evaluative analyses; discusses portfolio contents and analysis with student; establishes new goals; takes joint notes
Preparing explanation of portfolio and analysis of it to a particular audience	As occasion for allowing other audiences access arises	Thoughtfully fills out the form *About My Portfolio*	Keeps student advised as to when other audiences might be looking at the student's collection and who the viewer(s) will be
Reacting to a fellow student's paper or portfolio	When it is requested by a "partner" or other classmate	Completes the *Peer Evaluation: Any Project* form	Encourages collaboration whenever possible

Should I grade my students' portfolios?

Teachers might be tempted to grade portfolios to let students know that they are accountable for their work; teachers may also feel that a grade legitimizes—or at least recognizes—the time and effort that goes into successful portfolio assessment. Finally, many parents, school supervisors, and administrators will expect the teacher to grade the portfolio. These reasons notwithstanding, most portfolio experts recommend that portfolios not be graded. Keep in mind that the collection will contain papers that have been graded. A grade for the collection as a whole, however, risks undermining the goals of portfolio management. Grading portfolios may encourage students to include only their "best" work, and that practice may convey the message that student self-assessment is not taken seriously. Think about it: How would you feel if someone decided to incorporate your journal entries, your collection of ideas that interest you, and other notes and informal jottings into a package that was being rated and given a grade?

Who, besides the student and me, should see the portfolio?

This question raises some of the same concerns as the issue of grading portfolios. Teachers may feel some responsibility to let parents, a supervisor, the principal, and fellow faculty members know how the program is proceeding and what it shows about the progress of individuals or of the class as a whole. It is important to balance the benefits of showing portfolios to outside audiences against the possible adverse effects—the risk of inhibiting students, diminishing their sense of ownership, or invading their privacy. Above all, the primary aims of portfolio assessment must be kept in mind.

Following are some suggestions for showing portfolios, with respect to the audience involved.

PARENTS OR GUARDIANS Family members will almost certainly be viewing the portfolio in one form or another. If parents or other responsible adults are to view collections only on more formal occasions, such as back-to-school night or during unscheduled visits to the classroom, then students should be assisted in creating show portfolios. If, on the other hand, the teacher will show students' portfolios without the owners' knowledge or chance to review the contents beforehand, the teacher must tell students this at the beginning of the year. Warning students of these unscheduled viewings may qualify their sense of ownership; it can also intensify their audience awareness.

Another way to involve parents in portfolio management is to let students plan a workshop on portfolio management geared for parents and others who are interested. Or, as suggested earlier, have students cull their collections periodically and take the materials home for their parents to see.

Questions and Answers *(continued)*

Again, if portfolios will be shown to other educators, students should be made aware of this before they start to build their collections.

SCHOOL SUPERVISORS AND PRINCIPALS Students' portfolios can demonstrate to fellow educators how youngsters develop as language users, thinkers, and people; they can also show the kind of learning that is taking place in the classroom. When working portfolios are shown, they are usually selected at random from those kept in the class, and the owner's identity is masked. Show portfolios are usually prepared specifically for this purpose. Whether the teacher uses working or show collections (assuming the state or school system does not mandate one) may depend partly on whether she or he thinks the audience will be able to appreciate that the working collections show process.

CLASSMATES Students may review their peers' portfolios as part of the program's assessment. Even if a particular program does not include a formal peer review stage, remind students that peers may see their collections—either in the process of collaborative work or peer review, or because a student does not respect the privacy of others.

NEXT YEAR'S TEACHERS At the end of the school year, teachers can help students create a show portfolio for their next teacher or teachers. These portfolios should demonstrate the student's growth during the year and the potential of his or her best efforts. They should also indicate the most recent goals established by the teacher and the student, so that the new teacher knows how the student sees his or her language skills developing over the next year.

Encourage students to include finished projects as well as earlier drafts. Discuss what kinds of logs should be included—or have students prepare a brief report showing how goals have been met. A fresh table of contents would be useful, as would an explanation of what the show collection includes and what its purpose is. Teachers may want to let students make copies of some papers that they would also like to take home.

THE STUDENTS THEMSELVES At the end of the school year, portfolio contents can be sent home for parents to see and save, if they wish. Before doing this, teachers may wish to have students prepare a starter portfolio of ideas, writing, plans for reading, and so on, for next year.

How can I protect against the possible negative effects of allowing a wide variety of persons to see students' portfolios?

Whatever special reporting the teacher does with portfolios, he or she needs to offset any possible adverse effects by keeping the primary aims for portfolio assessment in mind:

Questions and Answers *(continued)*

- The overall goal of the program is to develop students as language users. That goal should become the focus of joint student/teacher evaluation of the student's progress.
- Another important goal is for students to develop a habit of self-assessment. That is why the collections must be readily available to students.
- The emphasis should be on examining the process by looking at the product and the way it is produced. Each portfolio should be a working collection containing notes, drafts, and records of the evaluation of its contents.
- The activities assessed should integrate reading, writing, speaking and listening, and viewing and representing.
- The portfolio should be controlled and owned by the student.
- The collections should include reactions to and applications of a variety of text and writing types—with a variety of purposes involving different audiences.

Arter, Judith A., and Spandel, Vicki. (1992) NCME instructional module: Using portfolios in instruction and assessment. *Educational Measurement: Issues and Practice,* 11 (1), pp. 36–44.
Practical, sequenced steps to a portfolio approach are presented as a training model.

Bishop, Wendy, and Crossley, Gay Lynn. (1993) Not only assessment: Teachers talk about writing portfolios. *Journal of Teaching Writing,* 12 (1), pp. 33–55.
This article shows how using writing-portfolio evaluation changes the way that teachers think about their roles, students, and students' writing. (Whole issue is on portfolios.)

Brown, Sarah. (Spring 1994) Validation of curriculum: Creating a multi-level book as a portfolio and more. *Exercise Exchange,* 39 (2), pp. 29–32.
Project portfolios represent various stages of student growth and writing achievement, result in a published volume of student writing, and validate a curriculum.

Cirincione, Karen M., and Michael, Denise. (October 1994) Changing portfolio process: One journey toward authentic assessment. *Language arts,* 71 (6), pp. 411–418.
Describes how one teacher matched authentic assessment to the instruction in her classroom. (Whole issue is on portfolios.)

Farr, Roger, and Farr, Beverly. (1990) *Language Arts Portfolio Teacher's Manual.* Integrated Assessment System. San Antonio: The Psychological Corporation.
This manual includes descriptions of how to use, rate, and interpret responses to the Integrated Assessment System and several chapters on developing and using portfolios.

Farr, Roger, and Tone, Bruce. (1994) *Portfolio and performance assessment: Helping students evaluate their progress as readers and writers.* Fort Worth: Harcourt Brace College Publishers.
Portfolio assessment and the development of performance assessments is explained in detail with numerous practical suggestions, checklists, and model forms. Working portfolios are recommended to promote students' analysis of their own language use.

Galbraith, Marian, et al. (1994) *Using portfolios to negotiate a rhetorical community.* Report Series 3.10. Albany, New York: National Research Center on Literature Teaching and Learning.
Teacher narration and discussion cover what is required in the negotiation and mentoring involved in becoming a co-assessor with the student of the student's work.

Grady, Emily. (Fall 1992) *The portfolio approach to assessment.* Fastback Series. Bloomington, Indiana: Phi Delta Kappa.
This booklet tells how to use portfolios to assess a wide range of student performance.

Hesse, Douglas. (1993) Portfolios and public discourse: Beyond the academic/personal writing polarity. *Journal of Teaching Writing,* 12 (1), pp. 1–12.
In addition to the writing students do for academic discourse and personal purposes, another kind, public discourse, makes portfolios highly effective. (Whole issue is on portfolios.)

Hewitt, Geof. (1995) *A portfolio primer: Teaching, collecting, and assessing student writing.* Portsmouth, New Hampshire: Heinemann.
This manual on portfolio assessment covers grades 3–12 and a broad range of key considerations, with generous examples from actual portfolios.

Palmer, Barbara C., et al. (1994) *Developing cultural literacy through the writing process: Empowering all learners.* Des Moines: Allyn and Bacon.
Emphasizing cultural literacy, this book addresses each stage of the writing process and treats portfolio assessment. Numerous model activities expand the writer's knowledge base and develop critical thinking.

Porter, Carol, and Cleland, Janell. (1995) *The portfolio as a learning strategy.* Portsmouth, New Hampshire: Heinemann.
Learning strategies involving portfolios and developing self-assessors are described.

Robbins, Sarah, et al. (November 1994) Using portfolio reflections to re-form instructional programs and build curriculum. *English Journal,* 83 (7), pp. 71–78.
English teachers in two schools rely on portfolio assessment to redesign their curricula.

Tierney, Robert J.; Carter, Mark A.; and Desai, Laura E. (1991) *Portfolio assessment in the reading-writing classroom.* Norwood, Massachusetts: Christopher-Gordon.
This presentation covers all aspects of portfolio assessment, relying on research and descriptions of actual implementation.

Valencia, Sheila W., and Place, Nancy. (May 1994) Portfolios: A process for enhancing teaching and learning, *The Reading Teacher,* 47 (8), pp. 666–669.
Aspects of a Bellevue (Washington) project helped teachers use portfolios effectively.

Valencia, Sheila W. (ed.), et al. (1994) *Authentic reading assessment: Practices and possibilities.* Newark, Delaware: International Reading Association.
Case studies describe authentic assessment in and beyond the classroom. Programs at particular schools and in particular states are detailed.

Summary of My Progress: Writing, Speaking, and Representing

Complete this form before sitting down with your teacher or a classmate to assess your overall progress, set goals, or discuss specific pieces of your work.

Grade : _____   **School year:** _____   **Date of summary:** _____

▶ **What work have I done so far this year?**	▶ **What project do I plan to work on next?**
Writing:	Writing:
Speaking:	Speaking:
Representing:	Representing:
▶ **What do I think of my progress?** What about my work has improved? What needs to be better?	▶ **Which examples of work are my favorites and why?**

Summary of My Progress: Writing, Speaking, and Representing *(continued)*

▶ **Which pieces of work need more revision, and what is needed?**

▶ **How has reading, listening, or viewing helped me in preparing for papers or other projects this year?**

▶ **What a classmate or the teacher thinks about my progress**

In writing—

In speaking—

In representing—

Summary of My Progress: Reading, Listening, and Viewing

Complete this form before sitting down with your teacher or a classmate to assess your overall progress; set goals; or discuss specific works you have read, listened to, or watched.

Grade: _____   **School year:** _____   **Date of summary:** _____

▶ **What have I read, listened to, or watched this year?**

Reading:

Listening:

Viewing:

▶ **What do I plan to read, listen to, or watch next?**

Reading:

Listening:

Viewing:

▶ **What do I think of my progress in understanding what I read, hear, or see?**

What about my skills has improved?

What needs to be better?

▶ **Which things that I've read, listened to, or watched are my favorites and why?**

Summary of My Progress: Reading, Listening, and Viewing *(continued)*

▶ **What topics in what I've read, listened to, or watched would I like to explore further? How would I explore these topics?**

▶ **How has writing, speaking, or making media products helped me to become a better reader, listener, or viewer?**

▶ **What a classmate or the teacher thinks about my progress**

In reading—

In listening—

In viewing—

Self-Evaluation: Any Project

Grade: _____ **School year:** _____ **Date of these comments:** _____

▶ **Title of work:** _____ **This is the** _____ **revision.**

The purpose of this work is—

The audience for this work is—

The things I like best about the work are—

The things about the work that do not satisfy me are—

The most difficult thing about writing or creating this work was—

Peer Evaluation: Any Project

Grade: _____   **School year:** _____   **Date of these comments:** _____

▶ **Person whose work I am reviewing:** _____   **Title of work:** _____

This is why the work is (or is not) appropriate for its intended audience:

This work could be improved by adding or explaining these things:

This work could be improved by cutting or replacing these things:

This work could be improved if the following things were reordered:

These are goals that could be considered for the next or a similar project:

These are the comments of _____

[Sign here if your comments are about someone else's paper]

My Self-Assessment Record

Use this form to evaluate specific pieces of your work, including papers, stories, oral reports, and video projects. Be sure to think carefully about your reasons for assigning ratings to each piece of work.

▶ **Ratings:**   Needs Improvement   Acceptable   Excellent
                            1   2   3   4   5

Title or description of paper or project:

Rating:

In deciding my rating, what strengths did I see in the paper or project?

What weaknesses did I see in the paper or project?

Title or description of paper or project:

Rating:

In deciding my rating, what strengths did I see in the paper or project?

What weaknesses did I see in the paper or project?

Title or description of paper or project:

Rating:

In deciding my rating, what strengths did I see in the paper or project?

What weaknesses did I see in the paper or project?

Goal-Setting for Reading, Writing, Speaking, Listening, Viewing, or Representing

GOAL	STEPS TO REACH GOAL	REVIEW OF PROGRESS
Reading Goals		
Writing Goals		

Goal-Setting for Reading, Writing, Speaking, Listening, Viewing, or Representing *(continued)*

▶ GOAL	▶ STEPS TO REACH GOAL	▶ REVIEW OF PROGRESS
Speaking and Listening Goals		
Viewing and Representing Goals		

Student-Teacher Conference Notes

Name of Teacher

▶ Student's notes	▶ Teacher's notes

Table of Contents: How My Portfolio is Organized

Decide on the major categories for work in your portfolio. Then, in the sections below, list the categories you have chosen. The works themselves may be papers, speech notecards, videotapes, multimedia products, or any work you and your teacher agree should be included. In choosing categories, consider organizing work by topic, by genre (essays, poems, stories, and so on), by chronology (work completed by month, for example), by level of difficulty (work that was less difficult, somewhat difficult, and more difficult), or according to another plan.

Grade: _____   **School year:** _____

WORK IN EACH SECTION	WHY I PUT THIS WORK IN THIS SECTION
Section 1:	
title:	
title:	
title:	
title:	
Section 2:	
title:	
title:	
title:	
title:	
Section 3:	
title:	
title:	
title:	
title:	

About My Portfolio

Use this form whenever you are preparing your portfolio for review by your teacher or another reader.

Grade: _____ **School year:** _____ **I began this portfolio on:** _____

▶ **How it is organized:**

_____

▶ **What I think it shows about my progress . . .**

_____

as a reader:

_____

as a writer:

_____

as a speaker:

_____

as a listener:

_____

as a viewer of media:

_____

as a maker of media products:

_____

as a critical thinker:

NAME _____ CLASS _____ DATE _____

About My Portfolio *(continued)*

▶ **Examples of My Best Work**

The best things I have read are—	Why I like them—

The best things I have written are—	Why I like them—

Other things in my portfolio that I hope you notice are— 1. 2. 3.	What they show—

TO PARENT OR GUARDIAN

The Portfolio: What Does It Show?

In the left column of the chart below, I have noted what I believe this portfolio shows about your student's development in areas such as reading, writing, speaking, listening, and critical viewing. The right column notes where you can look for evidence of that development.

    A prime objective in keeping portfolios is to develop in students a habit of analyzing and evaluating their work. This portfolio includes work that the student has collected over a period of time. The student has decided what to include but has been encouraged to include different types of writing, responses to reading, and evidence of other uses of language. Many of the writings included are accompanied by earlier drafts and plans that show how the work has evolved from a raw idea to a finished piece of writing. The inclusion of drafts is intended to reinforce to the student that using language entails a process of revision and refinement.

▶ I believe that this portfolio shows—	▶ To see evidence of this, please notice—

Teacher's signature_____

TO PARENT OR GUARDIAN

Response to the Portfolio

▶ Please answer any questions that seem important to you. Use the reverse side for any additional comments or questions.

Parent or Guardian_____ Date _____

What did you learn from the portfolio about your student's reading?

_____

_____

_____

What did you learn from the portfolio about your student's writing?

_____

_____

_____

Were you surprised by anything in the portfolio? Why?

_____

_____

What do you think is the best thing in the portfolio? What do you like about it?

_____

_____

_____

Do you have questions about anything in the portfolio? What would you like to know more about?

_____

_____

_____

What does the portfolio tell you about your student's progress as a writer, reader, and thinker?

_____

_____

_____

Do you think keeping a portfolio has had an effect on your student as a reader or writer—or in another way? If so, what?

_____

_____

_____

Is there anything missing from the portfolio that you would have liked or had expected to see? If so, what?

_____

_____

TEACHER'S REPORT

Student Awareness of Language as Process

Ratings:	1 = minimal progress	4 = more progress than expected
	2 = less progress than expected	5 = outstanding progress
	3 = some progress	

Processing strategy	Rating	Comments
Reads, writes, listens, and speaks with a specific purpose; can articulate these purposes		
Tends to appraise what he or she knows about the topic; applies available background knowledge to the task		
Considers clues that indicate what reading or listening may offer; thinks about or preplans expression		
Predicts what is coming next in text or oral presentation; considers what should come next (analyzes writer/speaker purpose and audience expectation)		
Pictures the meaning being made by reading, writing, listening, and speaking as the process unfolds		
Challenges the ideas, concepts, and details presented to see if they are making sense or are appropriate		
Considers strategy adjustments needed in order to construct clear meaning		
Seeks aid or advice when strategies do not resolve inability to construct clear meaning		

USE OF LANGUAGE ACROSS TIME PERIODS: TEACHER'S REPORT

Student Performance Graph

RATINGS: **10 = Outstanding Performance**   **8 = Good Performance**   **6 = Average to Above-Average Performance**
4 = Average to Below-Average Performance   **2 = Weak Performance**

Rating	1st Grading Period	2nd Grading Period	3rd Grading Period	4th Grading Period	5th Grading Period	6th Grading Period	Comments — How much overall progress has this student shown?
10							● Attitude toward using language
9							
8							✱ Involvement in improvement
7							
6							
5							✕ Amount/frequency of use
4							
3							✓ Effectiveness of use
2							
1							

Key Considerations in Growth of Language Use. Place the appropriate symbol for each category below opposite the rating for each period. Connect the symbols with different colored lines to create a chart.

● **Attitude toward using language**
How much does the student enjoy reading, writing, speaking, and listening?

✱ **Involvement in improvement**
How inclined is the student to self-assess, revise, and set new language-use goals?

✕ **Amount/frequency of use**
How often does the student read, write, and speak with a clear purpose?

✓ **Effectiveness of use**
How strong is the student's control of language conventions, diction, and style?
How effectively does the student use language to complete class work and communicate with others?

My Reading Record

Ratings:	✓✓✓✓ Terrific	✓✓✓ Good	✓✓ OK	✓ I didn't like it.

▶ Month/ Day	▶ Title, author fiction or nonfiction	▶ Notes about what I read	▶ Rating

NAME _____ CLASS _____ DATE _____

Inventory: Some Facts About My Reading

▶ Questions and answers about my reading	▶ More about my answers
How much do I read?	What kinds of things do I read?
How much do I read outside of school/at home?	What kind of reading do I do there?
Do I like to read?	Why or why not?
Of things I have read, these are my favorites:	Why do I like them best?
What topics do I like to read about?	Why do I like reading about these topics?
Is anything about reading difficult for me? What?	Why do I think it is difficult?
Has reading helped my writing?	Why do I think so?
How important is reading?	Why do I think this?

Inventory: Some Facts About My Reading Skills

Title: _____ **Author:** _____

▶ **Before I Read**

What can I predict will happen in the selection, having looked at illustrations, heads, charts, or maps?

_____

What is my purpose for reading (to interpret, to enjoy, to get information, to solve a problem, etc.)?

_____

What do I already know about the subject of this selection?

_____

How will I adjust my reading rate in order to better understand the selection or book? What kind of resources will I need as I read (dictionary, thesaurus, atlas, etc.)?

_____

▶ **While I Read**

How does what I already know connect with what I'm reading?

_____

What kinds of details do I find interesting? Why?

_____

What questions do I have? Do I need to adjust my predictions? Why?

_____

▶ **After I Read**

What is my reaction to the selection or book? Why?

_____

How were my predictions different from what I found in the selection or book? Why?

_____

Evaluation of My Reading Skills and Strategies: Narration/Description

DIRECTIONS Circle 0, 1, 2, or 3 below to indicate your evaluation of each item.

Evaluation Scale:	0 = Not at all	2 = Some of the time
	1 = I don't know	3 = Most or all of the time

BEFORE READING

1. Previewing the Text

- I determine the type of selection or book I am reading (biography, novel, short story, play, folk tale, myth, poem, or personal or descriptive essay).   0 1 2 3

- I look for difficult vocabulary words and decide on an appropriate reading rate.   0 1 2 3

2. Establishing a Purpose for Reading

- I identify my purpose for reading (to learn something new, to understand, to interpret, to enjoy, to solve problems).   0 1 2 3

3. Using Prior Knowledge

- I consider how my experiences might be connected with the text.   0 1 2 3

- I consider what I know about the author or the genre.   0 1 2 3

- I make predictions about what I will read.   0 1 2 3

DURING READING

1. Responding to the Text

- I think about how my experiences are related to what I'm reading.   0 1 2 3

- I take notes or use graphic organizers.   0 1 2 3

- I identify setting, characters or people, conflicts, and themes.   0 1 2 3

- I use context clues to help me determine meaning.   0 1 2 3

- I identify narrative and descriptive details (the sequence of events, sensory language, and so on).   0 1 2 3

- I make predictions about what will happen next in the text.   0 1 2 3

2. Monitoring Comprehension

- I re-read passages when my understanding breaks down.   0 1 2 3

- I read faster or more slowly based on my understanding of the text.   0 1 2 3

Evaluation of My Reading Skills and Strategies: Narration/Description *(continued)*

DIRECTIONS Circle 0, 1, 2, or 3 below to indicate your evaluation of each item.

| **Evaluation Scale:** | 0 = Not at all | 2 = Some of the time |
| | 1 = I don't know | 3 = Most or all of the time |

AFTER READING

1. Responding to the Text

▪ I reflect on the meaning of what I have read and think about how the meaning is connected to my knowledge and experience.	0 1 2 3
▪ I react to the selection or book and make my own interpretation.	0 1 2 3
▪ I evaluate my predictions about the reading.	0 1 2 3
▪ I discuss my thoughts about the selection or book with others.	0 1 2 3
▪ I extend my reading by choosing another related selection or book to read.	0 1 2 3
▪ I apply my reading to a paper or project.	0 1 2 3

2. Using Study Skills

▪ I summarize, paraphrase, or outline the selection or book.	0 1 2 3
▪ I can return to the text and scan for specific information.	0 1 2 3

Additional Comments:

SELF-EVALUATION

Evaluation of My Reading Skills and Strategies: Exposition

DIRECTIONS Circle 0, 1, 2, or 3 below to indicate your evaluation of each item.

Evaluation Scale:	0 = Not at all	2 = Some of the time
	1 = I don't know	3 = Most or all of the time

BEFORE READING

1. Previewing the Text

- I flip through the pages, looking at headings, illustrations, graphs, maps, charts, or other visuals. 0 1 2 3

- I determine the type of selection or book I am reading (textbook, manual, informative book or article about science, history, geography, etc.). 0 1 2 3

- I skim the text to examine the difficulty of vocabulary and decide on an appropriate reading rate. 0 1 2 3

2. Establishing a Purpose for Reading

- I set a purpose for reading (to learn something new, to understand, to interpret, to solve problems, to enjoy). 0 1 2 3

- I write down questions I want answered in the text (*who? what? where? when?* and *how?*). 0 1 2 3

3. Using Prior Knowledge

- I reflect on what I already know about the topic. 0 1 2 3

- I make predictions about what I will learn from the text and how the text will be organized. 0 1 2 3

DURING READING

1. Responding to the Text

- I think about what I already know about the topic and how the text supports or contradicts my knowledge. 0 1 2 3

- I identify main ideas and supporting details. 0 1 2 3

- I take notes or use graphic organizers to keep track of facts or examples that support the main idea. 0 1 2 3

- I use graphic organizers to help me sort out a reading's text structure. 0 1 2 3

- I note all problems and solutions or causes and effects. 0 1 2 3

Evaluation of My Reading Skills and Strategies: Exposition *(continued)*

DIRECTIONS Circle 0, 1, 2, or 3 below to indicate your evaluation of each item.

Evaluation Scale:	0 = Not at all	2 = Some of the time
	1 = I don't know	3 = Most or all of the time

Responding to the Text *(continued)*

- I summarize or paraphrase sections of the selection or book to check my understanding.   0   1   2   3

2. Monitoring Comprehension

- I re-read passages when my understanding breaks down.   0   1   2   3

- I read faster or more slowly based on my understanding of the text.   0   1   2   3

AFTER READING

1. Responding to the Text

- I react to the text and sum up what I've learned.   0   1   2   3

- I evaluate the credibility, or trustworthiness, of the source or text.   0   1   2   3

- I evaluate my predictions about the selection.   0   1   2   3

- I discuss my thoughts about the text with others.   0   1   2   3

- I extend my reading by choosing another related book, article, or other work to read.   0   1   2   3

- I apply my reading to a paper or project.   0   1   2   3

2. Using Study Skills

- I summarize, paraphrase, or outline the text's main ideas and supporting details.   0   1   2   3

- I return to the text and scan for specific information.   0   1   2   3

Additional Comments:

Evaluation of My Reading Skills and Strategies: Persuasion

DIRECTIONS Circle 0, 1, 2, or 3 below to indicate your evaluation of each item.

Evaluation Scale:	0 = Not at all 2 = Some of the time
	1 = I don't know 3 = Most or all of the time

BEFORE READING

1. Previewing the Text

- I flip through the pages, looking at headings, illustrations, graphs, maps, charts, or other visuals.   0   1   2   3

- I identify the type of selection I am reading (editorial, review, article, advertisement, etc.).   0   1   2   3

- I skim the text to find difficult vocabulary words and decide on an appropriate reading rate.   0   1   2   3

2. Establishing a Purpose for Reading

- I set a purpose for reading (to learn something new, to understand, to interpret, to be persuaded, to solve problems, to enjoy).   0   1   2   3

- I write down questions I want answered in the text (*who? what? where? when?* and *how?*).   0   1   2   3

3. Using Prior Knowledge

- I reflect on what I already know about the topic.   0   1   2   3

- I consider what my opinion on the topic might be.   0   1   2   3

- I reflect on what I already know about the author or publication.   0   1   2   3

- I make predictions about what I will learn from the text and what the author's opinion might be.   0   1   2   3

DURING READING

1. Responding to the Text

- I think about what I already know about the topic and how the text supports or contradicts my knowledge.   0   1   2   3

- I identify the author's position statement and supporting reasons and evidence.   0   1   2   3

- I distinguish between facts and opinions.   0   1   2   3

Evaluation of My Reading Skills and Strategies: Persuasion *(continued)*

Evaluation Scale:	0 = Not at all	2 = Some of the time
	1 = I don't know	3 = Most or all of the time

Responding to the Text *(continued)*

- I identify emotional and logical appeals, loaded language, and other persuasive techniques. — 0 1 2 3
- I can usually identify logical fallacies such as either-or reasoning, glittering generalities, and so on. — 0 1 2 3
- I take notes or use graphic organizers to keep track of facts, examples, or appeals that support the author's position. — 0 1 2 3
- I summarize or paraphrase sections of the text to confirm my understanding. — 0 1 2 3

2. Monitoring Comprehension

- I re-read passages when my understanding breaks down. — 0 1 2 3
- I read faster or more slowly based on my understanding of the text. — 0 1 2 3

AFTER READING

1. Responding to the Text

- I react to the text and formulate my own opinion. — 0 1 2 3
- I summarize the author's purpose and point of view. — 0 1 2 3
- I evaluate the credibility, or trustworthiness, of the source or text. — 0 1 2 3
- I evaluate my predictions about the text. — 0 1 2 3
- I discuss my thoughts about the text with others. — 0 1 2 3
- I extend my reading by choosing a related editorial or another work to read. — 0 1 2 3
- I apply my reading to a paper or project. — 0 1 2 3

2. Using Study Skills

- I summarize or outline the author's opinion and supporting details. — 0 1 2 3
- I return to the text and scan for specific information and arguments. — 0 1 2 3

Inventory: Some Facts About My Study Skills

▶ Questions and answers about my study skills	▶ More about my answers
How often do I study? Do I study at a special time and place?	How do I decide when and where to study?
Can I locate the table of contents, the glossary, and the index of my textbook?	How might these parts of the textbook help me study?
Do I preview or skim major sections of the text I'm reading?	How can previewing or skimming help me?
Do I review the maps, tables, and other graphic organizers in the texts that I study?	What help do these features provide?
Do I notice features such as bullets, headings, and subheadings?	How do these features help my understanding?
Do I use a dictionary, encyclopedia, or other reference materials in my studying?	Why or why not?
Do I ask myself questions about the text as I read? Do I use the study questions in my textbooks?	Why is asking questions important?

Inventory: Some Facts About My Study Skills *(continued)*

▶ Questions and answers about my study skills	▶ More about my answers
Do I use study strategies such as SQ3R or creating graphic organizers?	How do these strategies help me?
Do I practice making generalizations or drawing conclusions?	How does this help my understanding?
Do I distinguish between fact and opinion?	Why is it important to notice this difference?
Do I note causes and effects or problems and solutions in the texts I read?	Why is understanding these relationships helpful to my studying?
Do I make the necessary adjustments in my studying based on my reading rate?	Why is my reading rate important in studying?
Are my study habits successful?	Why or why not?

Progress in Reading

> ▶ **Ratings:**
>
> | | |
> |---|---|
> | 1 = minimal progress | 4 = more progress than expected |
> | 2 = less progress than expected | 5 = outstanding progress |
> | 3 = some progress | |

▶ Volume of reading	▶ Rating	▶ Comments
Compared with last progress report		
Amount student is reading during unscheduled school time		
Amount student is reading outside of school		
Has read from a variety of genres and sources such as diaries, newspapers, electronic texts, and speeches		

▶ Interests growing out of and promoting reading	▶ Rating	▶ Comments
Interest in some topics has intensified		
Has read texts on a variety of topics		
Is developing clear preferences in reading		
Shares ideas and stories from texts read		
Appears to be more questioning; turns to texts for answers		

Progress in Reading *(continued)*

Attitudes about reading	Rating	Comments
Reads assignments without resistance		
Talks about favorite books, stories, articles; cites texts read; reacts openly to what has been read in class		
Is actively involved in portfolio self-assessment of reading		
Has improved perception of self as a reader; demonstrates confidence with texts and ideas		

Applied comprehension	Rating	Comments
Relates reading to experience and background		
Reading appears to be promoting improvement in writing and speaking		
Expresses and shows appreciation for new ideas		

Reading strategies	Rating	Comments
Thinks of reading as a process		
Appears to read more fluently		
Has strategies to seek help if needed		
Has a growing lexicon/vocabulary		

TEACHER'S REPORT

Progress in Reading Skills

Ratings:	1 = minimal progress	4 = more progress than expected
	2 = less progress than expected	5 = outstanding progress
	3 = some progress	

Comprehension skills	Rating	Comments
Can identify main ideas and details		
After reading, can recall many details accurately		
Uses context clues to define difficult vocabulary		
Recognizes and understands common abbreviations, symbols, and acronyms		
Can identify correctly the antecedents of pronouns		
Can follow written instructions		
Can follow sequences of events		
Can identify and follow common text structures such as compare/contrast and cause/effect		
Recognizes common genres and can identify some distinguishing features of each		

Progress in Reading Skills *(continued)*

Interpretive skills	Rating	Comments
Can make logical predictions		
Can connect own knowledge and experience to the text		
Uses context clues to decipher meaning		
Can interpret character traits and relationships in fiction		
Can understand implied cause-and-effect relationships, implied main ideas, and implied sequences of events		
Can make generalizations and draw conclusions about a text		
Can decipher the meaning of abstract words and/or multiple-meaning words		
Can interpret figurative language		
Can accurately summarize a text		
Reads with an understanding of literary concepts such as plot and theme		
In nonfiction, can identify an author's purpose and point of view		
Can synthesize information from more than one source		

Progress in Reading Skills *(continued)*

Critical thinking skills	Rating	Comments
Can differentiate fact from opinion		
Can assess the credibility of an author		
Can recognize logical and emotional appeals and identify their purpose in a text		
Can recognize bias		
Can interpret persuasive and propaganda techniques and identify their purpose in a text		
Can detect fallacies in reasoning		
Can distinguish between relevant and irrelevant material in a text		

Record of My Writing

Ratings: ✓✓✓✓ One of my best!   ✓✓ OK, but not my best
              ✓✓✓ Better if I revise it   ✓ I don't like this one.

Month/ Day	Title and type of writing	Notes about this piece of writing	Rating

My Spelling Log

▶ Word	▶ My misspelling	▶ How to remember correct spelling

My Vocabulary Log

Put a circle around any of the words on your list that you often use in writing or speaking. Underline any of the words on your list that you frequently come across in reading.

> **Ratings:** ☆ = a word that you want to remember and use in writing or speaking
> + = a word you want to recognize when you come across it in reading

Word	Brief definition or synonym	Sentence the word was used in	Rating

Inventory: Some Facts About My Writing

▶ Questions and answers about my writing	▶ More about my answers
How often do I write?	What types of writing do I do?
Do I write outside of school/at home?	What kind of writing do I do there?
Do I like to write?	Why or why not?
Of the things I have written, I like these best:	Why do I like them best?
What topics do I like to write about?	Why do I like to write about these topics?
Is anything about writing difficult for me? What?	Why do I think it is difficult?
Does reading help me to be a better writer, or vice versa?	Why do I think this?
How important is learning to write well?	Why do I think this?

Evaluating Your Writing Process

Choose one paper from your portfolio. Track your writing process for that
paper by writing brief answers to these questions. Keep the questions and
your answers in your portfolio.

▶ **PREWRITING**

1. How did you decide on your subject?

2. Did you use any of the prewriting techniques you have learned in class? Which ones? How did
they work for you with this assignment?

3. Did you plan the organization of your paper before you started writing? Why or why not?

4. What did you like best about this stage of the assignment? What did you like least?

5. About how much time did you spend on this stage of the writing process?

▶ **WRITING**

6. What did you find easiest about writing your draft?

7. What did you find most difficult about writing your draft?

8. What was your main concern while writing the draft? Organization? Style? Development of ideas?
Something else? Why?

9. What did you like best about this stage of the writing process?

10. About how much time did you spend writing your draft?

Evaluating Your Writing Process *(continued)*

▶ EVALUATING AND REVISING

11. Did you receive feedback on your draft from anyone? If so, was the feedback helpful? Why or why not?

12. What did you think about your first draft? Why?

13. In this stage, did you make any major changes to your draft? Why or why not?

14. What did you like best about this stage of the writing process? What did you like least?

15. About how much time did you spend evaluating and revising your draft?

▶ PROOFREADING, PUBLISHING, AND REFLECTING

16. How did you proofread your paper and design its appearance? How long did this take?

17. Where did you publish your paper? If you published your paper by reading it aloud, who was your audience?

18. What did you like best about this stage of the writing process? What did you like least?

19. On which stage of the writing process did you spend the most time? How did spending this time affect the quality of your final paper?

20. What will you do differently the next time you write? What will you do the same way?

Assessing Your Writing Process: Analytic Scale

Choose one paper from your portfolio, preferably one for which you have your prewriting notes and all your drafts. Use the chart below to analyze your writing process. Circle the numbers that most clearly indicate how well your writing process meets the stated criteria. The lowest possible total score is 5, the highest, 20.

1 = Does not achieve these criteria

2 = Made some effort to meet these criteria but with little success

3 = Made a serious effort to meet these criteria and was fairly successful

4 = Clearly meets these criteria

Title of paper _____

▶ STAGE IN WRITING PROCESS	▶ CRITERIA FOR EVALUATION	▶ RATING
Prewriting	■ Used prewriting techniques to find and limit subject and to gather details about subject ■ Organized details in a reasonable way	1 2 3 4
Writing	■ Got most of ideas down on paper in a rough draft	1 2 3 4
Revising	■ Did complete peer or self-evaluation ■ Found ways to improve content, organization, and style of rough draft ■ Revised by adding, cutting, replacing, and moving material	1 2 3 4
Proofreading	■ Corrected errors in spelling, grammar, usage, punctuation, capitalization, and manuscript form	1 2 3 4
Publishing and Reflecting	■ Produced a clean final copy in proper form ■ Shared the piece of writing with others ■ Reflected on the writing process and on the paper's strengths and weaknesses	1 2 3 4

Additional Comments:

Evaluating and Revising Your Draft

Read through your draft using the following five steps as a guide. Answer each question fully and thoughtfully.

Title of paper _____

STEP 1: THINKING ABOUT YOUR READERS

How do you want your readers to react to your paper?

Read through your paper quickly without stopping. Then, state what you think the readers' reactions will be.

If the readers' reactions are likely to be different than the reaction you want, what do you need to change in the paper?

STEP 2: LOOKING AT YOUR INTRODUCTION

Look closely at the introduction to your paper. What does the introduction do to capture the readers' interest?

What do you like best about your introduction?

What do you like least?

What might you add, cut, replace, or reorder to strengthen your introduction?

Evaluating and Revising Your Draft *(continued)*

> **STEP 3: LOOKING AT THE BODY**

Read carefully through the body of your paper. What main points or ideas do you want your readers to understand?

Do you think the reader will consider the order of your ideas or points logical? Explain.

What examples of vivid, precise, or persuasive language do you find in the body of the essay?

Does this assignment call for examples and facts? If so, what examples and facts have you used?

Where might additional facts and examples be helpful?

Do any facts or examples seem unrelated or unnecessary? Why?

What might you add, cut, replace, or reorder to strengthen the body of the paper?

Evaluating and Revising Your Draft *(continued)*

STEP 4: LOOKING AT THE CONCLUSION

Look closely at the conclusion of your paper. What does the conclusion do to bring the paper to a satisfactory close?

What do you like best about your conclusion?

What do you like least?

What might you add, cut, replace, or reorder to strengthen your conclusion?

STEP 5: HEARING HOW THE PAPER SOUNDS

Read your paper aloud. Which sentences sound especially good to you?

Which sentences seem awkward, wordy, or unclear?

What words or phrases might you add, cut, replace, or reorder to strengthen those sentences?

Checklist: Evaluating and Revising Your Draft

Revise your paper until you can answer *yes* to each of the following questions.
Add, cut, replace, or reorder material in your paper as necessary.

Title of paper _____

Content	Yes	No
Does the introduction grab the reader's interest?		
Is the introduction clear and logical?		
From the beginning of the paper to the end, are the subject and purpose of the paper clear?		
Is the body of the paper well developed?		
Is each main point in the paper elaborated with facts, details, or other support?		
Is the paper free of unrelated or unnecessary ideas?		
Is the paper interesting?		
Does the paper end in a way that is satisfying to the reader?		
Does the paper achieve its purpose? (Before you answer, take a moment to recall the paper's purpose as clearly as possible.)		
Organization	**Yes**	**No**
Are the ideas and details arranged in a clear and logical order?		
Have transitions been used to make clear the relationships between sentences and paragraphs?		
Style	**Yes**	**No**
Is every sentence in the paper clear and smoothly written?		
Is the language of the paper appropriate for its audience and purpose?		
Have you avoided choppy and wordy sentences? Have you varied your sentence lengths and structures?		

Additional Notes:

Evaluating Your Content and Organization

Writer's name _____ **Title of paper** _____

▶**Introduction**

The best thing about the introduction is—

To improve the introduction, the writer might—

_____

▶**Body**

The two best things about the body are—

The body's organization is or is not clear because—

To improve the body, the writer might—

_____

▶**Conclusion**

The best thing about the conclusion is—

To improve the conclusion, the writer might—

_____

▶**Overall Evaluation**

What does this writer do best of all?

Check the element that the writer should concentrate most on when revising.

_____ Interest Level   _____ Style   _____ Organization   _____ Development of Ideas

Evaluating Your Audience and Purpose

Writer's name _____ **Title of paper** _____

▶ **STEP 1: Evaluating for Audience**

Who is the intended audience of the paper?

What information, ideas, or attitudes are they likely to have about the subject of the paper?

Has the writer taken the audience's knowledge, ideas, and attitudes into account? How can you tell?

Considering the audience, does the writer need to add material to the paper or delete material from the paper? If so, what?

▶ **STEP 2: Evaluating for Purpose**

What is the purpose of the paper?

What are some characteristics that papers with that purpose usually have?

Which of those characteristics does this paper have? Give examples.

Which of those characteristics (if any) are missing from this paper? What reasons might the writer have for not including those characteristics?

How successful is the writer in achieving the purpose? What might help the writer more fully meet the purpose?

▶ **STEP 3: Overall Evaluation**

What is the most important thing the writer needs to do to be certain of achieving his or her purpose with this audience?

Revising: Your Response as a Reader

Writer's name _____ **Title of paper** _____

1. Which part of the paper did you find most interesting? Why? _____

_____

_____

2. Which part of the paper might the writer make more interesting? _____

_____

How would you suggest that the writer do this? _____

_____

3. What is the writer's purpose? How can you tell? _____

_____

Do you think the writer is successful in achieving the purpose? Explain. _____

_____

_____

4. Are any parts of the paper difficult to read or understand? If so, which ones and why?

_____

_____

5. Does the paper need further editing and proofreading? Explain.

_____

_____

6. When the writer revises, is there anything that he or she definitely should not change?

_____

_____

7. Suggest two specific things the writer could do to improve the paper.

_____

_____

8. Tell the writer what he or she did well or what you will remember about this paper.

_____

_____

Four-Point Analytic Scale for Revising

Read the following list of criteria for good writing. Then, with these criteria in mind, read your classmate's paper. Finally, for each criterion, rate the writing assignment from 1 to 4. The lowest possible total score is 12, the highest, 48.

1 = Does not achieve this standard

2 = Shows some effort to meet this standard but with little success

3 = Shows a serious effort to meet this standard and was fairly successful

4 = Clearly meets this standard

Be ready to discuss your evaluation with the writer and to make suggestions for revision.

Writer's name _____   **Title of paper** _____

Criteria for Evaluation	Rating			
▪ The writing is interesting.	1	2	3	4
▪ The writing achieves its purpose.	1	2	3	4
▪ The writing contains enough details.	1	2	3	4
▪ The writing does not contain unrelated ideas.	1	2	3	4
▪ The ideas and details are arranged in an effective order.	1	2	3	4
▪ The connections between ideas and between sentences are clear.	1	2	3	4
▪ The writer's meaning is clear throughout.	1	2	3	4
▪ The language fits the audience and purpose of the piece of writing.	1	2	3	4
▪ The sentences read smoothly.	1	2	3	4
▪ The paper is free (or almost free) of problems in grammar and usage.	1	2	3	4
▪ The paper is free (or almost free) of problems in punctuation, capitalization, and spelling.	1	2	3	4
▪ The paper is free (or almost free) of problems in manuscript form.	1	2	3	4
Total:				

General Analytic Scale

The points possible for each of the twelve criteria listed in the chart may vary depending on the writing assignment that is being evaluated. Your teacher may give you the points possible for each category. Or, for some assignments, your teacher may give you the responsibility of deciding the points possible.

After you have filled out the **Points Possible** column, read the paper (your own or a classmate's) carefully and thoughtfully. Complete the **Points Given** column and tally the score.

Writer's name _____   **Title of paper** _____

CRITERIA FOR EVALUATION	Points Possible	Points Given
Content		
Is the writing interesting?		
Does the writing achieve its purpose?		
Are there enough details?		
Are the ideas related to the topic?		
Organization		
Are ideas and details arranged in an effective order?		
Are the connections between ideas, sentences, and paragraphs clear?		
Style		
Is the meaning of each sentence clear?		
Are the language and tone appropriate for the audience, topic, and purpose?		
Do sentences read smoothly?		
Grammar and Usage		
Is the paper relatively free of problems in grammar and usage?		
Punctuation, Capitalization, and Spelling		
Is the paper relatively free of problems in punctuation, capitalization, and spelling?		
Manuscript Form		
Is the paper relatively free of problems in manuscript form?		
Total Points:		

Four-Point Analytic Scale: General

Circle the numbers that most clearly indicate how well the paper meets the stated criteria. Total the numbers circled. The lowest possible score is 15, the highest, 60.

1 = The paper clearly does not achieve this standard.

2 = The paper indicates that the writer has made some effort to meet this standard but with little success.

3 = The paper indicates that the writer has made a serious effort to meet this standard and that he or she has been fairly successful.

4 = The paper clearly meets this standard.

Writer's name _____ **Title of paper** _____

Content

▪ The writing is likely to interest the intended audience.	1	2	3	4
▪ The writing has a clear purpose and achieves that purpose.	1	2	3	4
▪ The writing is unified and clear.	1	2	3	4
▪ The subject has been as completely explored and elaborated as possible.	1	2	3	4
▪ The writing does not contain unrelated or distracting details.	1	2	3	4

Organization

▪ The writing has a clear structure.	1	2	3	4
▪ Ideas and details are arranged in an effective and logical order.	1	2	3	4
▪ The connections between and among ideas are clear.	1	2	3	4

Style

▪ The language suits the topic, audience, purpose, and occasion.	1	2	3	4
▪ The sentences are graceful and not awkward.	1	2	3	4
▪ The paper avoids wordiness, clichés, jargon, and other style problems.	1	2	3	4
▪ The writer's meaning is clear throughout.	1	2	3	4

Grammar, Usage, and Mechanics

▪ The paper is relatively free of problems in grammar and usage.	1	2	3	4
▪ The paper is relatively free of errors in spelling and mechanics.	1	2	3	4
▪ The paper follows correct manuscript form.	1	2	3	4

Total: _____

Open Analytic Scale

Writer's name _____ **Title of paper** _____

EVALUATION CRITERIA	Points Possible	Points Given
Content:	20 *or* _____	
Organization:	20 *or* _____	
Style:	20 *or* _____	
Grammar and Usage:	20 *or* _____	
Spelling, Punctuation, and Manuscript Form:	20 *or* _____	
Total Points:	100	

Analytic Scale: A Life Experience

Read the autobiographical incident (your own or a classmate's) carefully and thoughtfully. Then, read each of the following criteria and complete the **Points Given** column. When you are finished, tally the score.

Writer's name _____ Title of paper _____

CRITERIA FOR EVALUATION	Points Possible	Points Given
Organization		
Are the events arranged in chronological order?	5	
Are the events connected using transitions?	5	
Is the narrative's organization easy to follow?	5	
Content		
Does the introduction engage the reader?	5	
Does the writer provide background information?	10	
Do the first, second, and third paragraphs describe the beginning, middle, and end, respectively, of the incident?	10	
Does the essay include both action and sensory details?	10	
Does the writer share his or her thoughts and feelings?	10	
Does the conclusion explain how the incident affected the writer?	10	
Style		
Does the narrative contain exact verbs?	5	
Is the tone of the narrative personal?	5	
Is the writer's meaning clear throughout the narrative?	5	
Grammar, Usage, and Mechanics		
Is the narrative relatively free of grammar and usage problems?	5	
Is the narrative relatively free of spelling and mechanics errors?	5	
Does the writer correctly capitalize proper nouns?	5	
Total Points:	100	

Analytic Scale: A Newspaper Article

Circle the numbers that clearly indicate how well the news article meets the stated criteria. Total the numbers circled. The lowest possible score is 15, the highest, 60.

1 = The article clearly does not achieve this standard.

2 = The article indicates that the writer has made some effort to meet this standard but with little success.

3 = The article indicates that the writer has made a serious effort to meet this standard and that he or she has been fairly successful.

4 = The article clearly meets this standard.

Writer's name _____ **Title of paper** _____

▶ **Organization**					
The details of the event are arranged from most important to least important.	1	2	3	4	
Connections between the details are clear.	1	2	3	4	
The article's organization is easy to follow.	1	2	3	4	
▶ **Content**					
The lead paragraph answers the *5W-How?* questions.	1	2	3	4	
The news event is newsworthy.	1	2	3	4	
The article explains the effects of the event.	1	2	3	4	
The writer shows people's reactions to the event.	1	2	3	4	
The writer includes quotations that support the details of the article.	1	2	3	4	
The article does not show the writer's opinions of the event.	1	2	3	4	
▶ **Style**					
The article uses sentences of varying length.	1	2	3	4	
The writer's tone and voice are appropriate for the purpose and audience.	1	2	3	4	
The writer's meaning is clear throughout the article.	1	2	3	4	
▶ **Grammar, Usage, and Mechanics**					
The article is relatively free of grammar and usage problems.	1	2	3	4	
The article is relatively free of spelling and mechanics errors.	1	2	3	4	
The writer uses correct punctuation to avoid run-on sentences when combining sentences	1	2	3	4	

Total Points: _____

Analytic Scale: A "How-To" Article

Read the "how-to" paper (your own or a classmate's) carefully and thoughtfully. Then, read each of the following criteria and complete the **Points Given** column. When you are finished, tally the score.

Writer's name _____ Title of paper _____

CRITERIA FOR EVALUATION	Points Possible	Points Given
Organization		
Are the steps arranged in chronological order?	10	
Is the organization easy to follow?	5	
Content		
Does the introduction introduce the product and engage the reader?	5	
Does the writer give a reason for making the product?	10	
Does the body give a list of needed materials?	10	
Does the writer use specific language to elaborate on each step?	10	
Does the conclusion restate the reason for making the product?	10	
Does the conclusion give suggestions on how to use the product?	10	
Style		
Do the instructions contain transitional words?	5	
Are the writer's directions clear throughout the instructions?	10	
Grammar, Usage, and Mechanics		
Are the instructions relatively free of grammar and usage problems?	5	
Are the instructions relatively free of spelling and mechanics errors?	5	
Does the writer correctly use commas in a series?	5	
Total Points:	100	

Analytic Scale: A Comparison-Contrast Essay

Use the chart below to evaluate a comparison-contrast essay. Circle the numbers that most clearly indicate how well the essay meets the stated criteria. The lowest possible total score is 11, the highest, 44.

1 = Does not achieve this standard

2 = Made some effort to meet this standard but with little success

3 = Made a serious effort to meet this standard and was fairly successful

4 = Clearly meets this standard

Writer's name _____   **Title of paper** _____

WRITING ELEMENT	CRITERIA FOR EVALUATION	RATING			
Organization	■ Details are arranged using block style.	1	2	3	4
	■ The essay's organization is easy to follow and understand.	1	2	3	4
Content	■ The introduction grabs the readers' attention and clearly states the main idea of the essay.	1	2	3	4
	■ The body paragraphs clearly explain how the two subjects are similar or different.	1	2	3	4
	■ The essay includes relevant details that support the points of comparison.	1	2	3	4
	■ The conclusion summarizes the information and restates the thesis.	1	2	3	4
Style	■ The essay contains a variety of sentences—short and long.	1	2	3	4
	■ The writer's tone is appropriate for an informative purpose.	1	2	3	4
Grammar, Usage, and Mechanics	■ The essay is relatively free of grammar and usage mistakes.	1	2	3	4
	■ The essay is relatively free of spelling and mechanics errors.	1	2	3	4
	■ The essay uses comparative modifiers correctly.	1	2	3	4
	Total Points:		_____		

Analytic Scale: A Book Review

Rate how well the book review meets the following criteria on a scale of 1 to 5, with 1 being the lowest rating and 5 being the highest. When you are finished, add the numbers to calculate a total score. The lowest possible score is 12, the highest, 60.

Writer's name _____ **Title of paper** _____

Criteria for Evaluation: **Rating (1 to 5):**

1. The introduction grabs the audience's attention. _____

2. The introduction gives the title and author of the book. _____

3. The summary includes information about the book's setting and main character. _____

4. The summary gives plot details in chronological order. _____

5. The summary uses transitions to show how the major events are connected. _____

6. The conclusion includes a clear evaluation of the book, with at least one reason for the writer's opinion. _____

7. The writer concludes his or her report with a recommendation. _____

8. The writer's tone is appropriate for the purpose and audience. _____

9. The analysis is free of clichés. _____

10. The analysis is relatively free of grammar and usage problems. _____

11. The analysis is relatively free of spelling and mechanics errors. _____

12. The writer has correctly used and punctuated appositives. _____

Total Points: _____

PEER AND SELF-EVALUATION

Analytic Scale: A Research Report

Use the following questions to evaluate a research paper. Read the paper carefully. Then, award points for each criterion. Finally, add the points in the **Points Given** column to determine a final score.

Writer's name _____ **Title of paper** _____

CRITERIA FOR EVALUATION	Points Possible	Points Given
▪ Does the introduction get the reader's attention?	5	
▪ Does the writer provide a main idea statement that clearly identifies the topic and major points of the report?	10	
▪ Does each body paragraph explain only one part of the topic?	10	
▪ Does each paragraph contain facts that give clear information about the topic?	10	
▪ Does the report include information from at least three sources?	10	
▪ Does the conclusion restate the report's main idea?	5	
▪ Is the information in each paragraph in the writer's own words?	10	
▪ Does the writer include a properly formatted Works Cited list?	10	
▪ Is the organization of the paper easy to follow?	5	
▪ Is the writer's tone appropriate for the audience and purpose?	5	
▪ Does the writer use precise nouns?	5	
▪ Is the paper relatively free of grammar and usage problems?	5	
▪ Is the paper relatively free of spelling and mechanics errors?	5	
▪ Does the writer correctly capitalize and punctuate titles?	5	
Total Points:	100	

Analytic Scale: A Persuasive Letter

Circle the numbers on the scales that indicate how well the persuasive letter meets the stated criteria. Total the numbers circled. The lowest possible score is 15, the highest, 45.

> **Ratings:** 1 = Does not meet this standard
> 2 = Made some effort at meeting this standard
> 3 = Clearly meets this standard

Writer's name _____ **Title of paper** _____

Organization

- Reasons are arranged in a logical order.   1   2   3
- The letter's organization is easy to follow.   1   2   3

Content

- The introduction grabs the reader's attention.   1   2   3
- The writer includes a clear opinion statement.   1   2   3
- The writer gives at least two reasons to support his or her opinion.   1   2   3
- Each reason is supported by at least one fact or example.   1   2   3
- Facts and examples are elaborated upon through explanation.   1   2   3
- The conclusion summarizes the reasons.   1   2   3
- The conclusion gives a reasonable and specific call to action.   1   2   3

Style

- The letter is free of stringy sentences.   1   2   3
- The writer's tone is appropriate for the audience and purpose.   1   2   3
- The writer's meaning is clear throughout the paper.   1   2   3

Grammar, Usage, and Mechanics

- The letter is relatively free of grammar and usage problems.   1   2   3
- The letter is relatively free of spelling and mechanics errors.   1   2   3
- The writer correctly punctuates possessive nouns and pronouns.   1   2   3

Total Points: _____

Proofreading Review

Proofread your paper using each of the following steps. Put a check by each
step after you complete it.

_____   **1.** Read the paper backward word by word.

_____   **2.** Make a large card with a one- or two-inch-sized strip cut into it
             and read every word in the paper, one at a time, through the hole.

_____   **3.** Read the first sentence in your paper carefully. Put your left index
             finger on the punctuation mark that signals the end of that sentence.
             Now, put your right index finger on the punctuation mark that ends
             the second sentence. Carefully read the material between your
             fingers; then, move your left index finger to the end of the second
             sentence, your right to the end of the third sentence and read
             carefully. Keep moving your fingers until you have carefully
             examined each sentence in the paper.

List the mistakes you discovered when proofreading.

_____

_____

_____

_____

_____

_____

_____

_____

_____

_____

_____

_____

Proofreading Checklist

Read through the paper and then mark the following statements either **T** for true or **F** for false. Return the paper and checklist to the writer. Give the writer time to locate and correct the errors. After the writer has done his or her best to correct the paper, offer to assist if your help is needed.

Writer's name _____   **Title of paper**_____

_____ 1. The paper is neat.

_____ 2. Each sentence begins with a capital letter.

_____ 3. Each sentence ends with a period, question mark, or exclamation mark.

_____ 4. Each sentence is complete. Each has a subject and a predicate and expresses a complete thought.

_____ 5. Run-on sentences are avoided.

_____ 6. A singular verb is used with each singular subject and a plural verb with each plural subject.

_____ 7. Nominative case pronouns such as *I* and *we* are used for subjects; objective case pronouns such as *me* and *us* are used for objects.

_____ 8. Singular pronouns are used to refer to singular nouns, and plural pronouns are used to refer to plural nouns.

_____ 9. Indefinite pronoun references are avoided.

_____ 10. Each word is spelled correctly.

_____ 11. Frequently confused verbs such as *lie/lay, sit/set, rise/raise, all ready/already*, and *fewer/less* are used correctly.

_____ 12. Double negatives are avoided.

_____ 13. All proper nouns and proper adjectives are capitalized.

_____ 14. Word endings such as *–s, –ing*, and *–ed* are included where they should be.

_____ 15. No words have been accidentally left out or accidentally written twice.

_____ 16. Each paragraph is indented.

_____ 17. Apostrophes are used correctly with contractions and possessive nouns.

_____ 18. Commas or pairs of commas are used correctly.

_____ 19. Dialogue is punctuated and capitalized correctly.

_____ 20. Any correction that could not be rewritten or retyped is crossed out with a single line.

My Record of Proofreading Corrections

Keeping a record of your mistakes can be helpful. For the next few writing assignments, list the errors you, your teacher, or your peers find in your work. If you faithfully use this kind of record, you'll find it easier to avoid troublesome errors.

Writer's name _____ **Title of paper** _____

Write sentences that contain errors in grammar or usage here.   **Write corrections here.**

_____   _____

_____   _____

_____   _____

_____   _____

_____   _____

_____   _____

_____   _____

_____   _____

Write sentences that contain errors in mechanics here.   **Write corrections here.**

_____   _____

_____   _____

_____   _____

_____   _____

_____   _____

_____   _____

_____   _____

Write misspelled words and corrections here.

_____ _____   _____ _____

_____ _____   _____ _____

_____ _____   _____ _____

_____ _____   _____ _____

_____ _____   _____ _____

SELF-EVALUATION

My Multiple-Assignment Proofreading Record

DIRECTIONS: When your teacher returns a corrected writing assignment, write the title or topic on the appropriate vertical line at right. Under the topic, record the number of errors you made in each area. Use this sheet when you proofread your next assignment, taking care to check those areas in which you make frequent mistakes.

TITLE OR TOPIC OF ASSIGNMENT

Type of Error								
Sentence Fragments								
Run-on Sentences								
Subject-Verb Agreement								
Pronoun Agreement								
Incorrect Pronoun Form								
Use of Double Negative								
Comparison of Adjectives and Adverbs								
Confusing Verbs								
Irregular Verbs								
Noun Plurals and Possessives								
Capitalization								
Spelling								
End Punctuation								
Apostrophes								
Confusing Words								
Quotation Marks and Italics								
Comma or Paired Commas								

My Self-Assessment Record

Ratings:	Needs Improvement		Acceptable		Excellent
	1	2	3	4	5

What I am judging (title or description)	What I like:	What I don't like:	Rating

Evaluating Presentation and Format

The presentation of your paper can enhance your message, making your text more accessible and pleasing to your reader. Use the following rating scale to evaluate the presentation of your own paper or a classmate's.

Ratings:	Needs Improvement		Acceptable		Excellent
	1	2	3	4	5

Rating   Presentation Criteria

_____   **1.** If handwritten, the slant of the letters is consistent, the letters are clearly formed, and spacing is even between words.
Comments:

_____   **2.** If word processed, there is appropriate use of boldface, italics, underlining, font and font sizes. No more than two or three different fonts are used; in addition, the font styles are used consistently.
Comments:

_____   **3.** There is a good balance between the white space on the page (spacing, margins) and the text. The intended reader can easily focus on the text; pages are not cluttered or completely filled with text.
Comments:

_____   **4.** The use of a title, subheadings, page numbers, bullets, and other features make it easy for the reader to find and understand the information presented in the paper. All headings and bullets clarify the arrangement of ideas.
Comments:

_____   **5.** All illustrations, charts, graphs, maps, tables, and other graphics work well with the text. The visuals clarify and support key points in the text.
Comments:

_____   **6.** If a Works Cited or Works Consulted list is used, the citations are complete and consistently follow the Modern Language Association (MLA) style or the style assigned by the teacher.
Comments:

TEACHER'S REPORT

Progress in Writing

Ratings:
1 = minimal progress
2 = less progress than expected
3 = some progress
4 = more progress than expected
5 = outstanding progress

Volume of Writing	Rating	Comments
Compared with last progress report		
Amount the student is writing during unscheduled school time		
Amount student is writing outside of school		
Writes in different genres		
Writes with a variety of purposes		
Writes for a variety of audiences		

Writing Process	Rating	Comments
Has obvious purposes for writing; writes about interests and background		
Demonstrates audience awareness		
Plans written efforts when appropriate		
Revises work		
Self-assesses using his or her portfolio collection		

Progress in Writing *(continued)*

Writing Strategies	Rating	Comments
Focuses effectively on topics		
Organizes material effectively		
Handles details effectively		
Writes with clarity and directness		
Diction—uses words effectively; makes varied and purposeful choices		
Appreciates the beauty and impact of language		
Demonstrates variety in the development of ideas		
Uses a variety of sentence structures		
Is developing a personal style		

Writing Mechanics	Rating	Comments
Uses words accurately and precisely		
Follows conventions of grammar and usage		
Punctuates and constructs sentences correctly		
Spells correctly		

Progress in Writing Conventions

Ratings: 1 = continues to have a problem in this area
        2 = has made gains in correcting problem
        3 = student does this correctly

Sentence Formation	Rating
Writes complete sentences; avoids fragments, unless used purposefully	
Avoids run-on sentences	
Avoids misplaced or dangling modifiers	
Uses subordination and coordination correctly in sentences; does not connect unrelated clauses	
Uses parallel structure	
Does not omit necessary words, phrases, or clauses	

Usage	Rating
Uses correct subject-verb agreement	
Uses tense correctly and consistently	
Uses auxiliary verbs and inflected verbs correctly	
Pronouns agree with their antecedents	
Pronouns are correct in nominative, possessive, and objective cases	
Avoids indefinite pronoun reference	
Uses apostrophes correctly	
Avoids confusion of word groups (adjectives with adverbs, singular with plural)	
Avoids double negatives	
Avoids confusion of comparative and superlative degrees	
Avoids inappropriate homonyms	

Mechanics and Spelling	Rating
Uses capitalization rules correctly	
Uses end punctuation correctly	
Uses internal punctuation correctly	
Uses and formats paragraphs appropriately	
Can spell common and advanced words	

Brief comments:

Creating a Guide for Evaluating Papers

Check off each step as the class completes the activity.

_____ **1.** The students read their papers aloud. No one comments until everyone has read.

_____ **2.** The students decide what the papers have in common that makes them good.

_____ **3.** The students list the four most important criteria in the form of complete sentences. Each sentence begins "A good paper has (or does) . . ."

_____ **4.** The students review the writing assignment to decide if they want to include additional criteria, and any new criteria are added to the list.

_____ **5.** Working independently, in pairs, or in peer groups, the students evaluate their papers using the criteria as a guide, indicating how successful their papers have been in achieving each goal (1 = Not at all successful, 2 = Somewhat successful, 3 = Almost totally successful, 4 = Totally successful).

As a final step, students might meet in small groups to ask peer advice on how to rewrite in order to achieve a four (4) on all criteria.

Additional instructions or comments:

My Speaking and Listening Record

Use this record for both formal and informal speaking and listening experiences. Log at least one experience a week.

> **Ratings:** ✓✓✓✓ This was very important!   ✓✓ I learned a little.
> ✓✓✓ Worth doing/remembering   ✓ I wasted my time.

Date:

What I said, heard, or saw:

Notes about why this experience was or was not important, interesting, or useful:

Rating:

Date:

What I said, heard, or saw:

Notes about why this experience was or was not important, interesting, or useful:

Rating:

Date:

What I said, heard, or saw:

Notes about why this experience was or was not important, interesting, or useful:

Rating:

Inventory: Some Facts About My Speaking

Questions and answers about my speaking	More about my answers
How do I feel about speaking to friends?	What do I like to discuss with them?
How do I feel about talking to adults?	Why do I feel this way?
How do I feel about reciting or speaking to the class?	Why do I feel this way?
What is the most difficult thing about speaking?	Why is it difficult?
What techniques have I learned to improve my speaking?	How do I use these techniques with friends or in class?

Inventory: Some Facts About My Listening

▶ **Questions and answers about my listening**	▶ **More about my answers**
What kinds of music do I like to listen to?	Why do I like them?
What TV shows and movies are my favorites?	What do I like about them?
How well do I listen in school?	How much do I learn by listening?
Do I listen carefully to what my friends say?	What do I learn from them?
When is it difficult for me to listen?	What makes it difficult?
How do I use the praise and suggestions of others to improve my skills?	How do I feel about getting praise or suggestions for improvement?

Evaluating My Critical Listening

To evaluate your ability to listen critically, answer the following questions about an oral presentation you recently heard. Compare your answers with those of other classmates who also heard the presentation.

1. What was the speaker's purpose? _____

   _____

2. What main points did the speaker make? _____

   _____

   _____

3. What examples, details, illustrations, or facts do you remember from the presentation? _____

   _____

   _____

   _____

4. Explain why you think the speaker chose to use the examples, illustrations, or other things you listed in your answer to Question 3. Be specific about as many items as you can. _____

   _____

   _____

   _____

   _____

5. How were the points in the presentation ordered—order of importance, logical order, or some other pattern? Was the organization effective? _____

   _____

   _____

   _____

   _____

6. As the speaker spoke, were you able to draw conclusions and make predictions about what would come next? Were they accurate? Why or why not? _____

   _____

   _____

   _____

   _____

Evaluating My Critical Listening *(continued)*

7. As the speaker spoke, were you able to make connections to your own experience or prior knowledge? Why or why not? _____

_____

_____

8. Did you detect any bias in the speech? If so, what? _____

_____

_____

9. What emotional appeals or other persuasive techniques did you hear? _____

_____

_____

_____

10. Why do you think the speaker was or was not credible, or trustworthy, to speak on this issue?

_____

_____

11. If visual aids were used, were they effective? Why or why not? _____

_____

_____

12. What did the speaker say that puzzled or bothered you? How did this affect your reaction to the presentation? _____

_____

_____

13. What do you think are the strengths of the presentation? _____

_____

_____

_____

14. Were there any weaknesses? If so, what were they? _____

_____

_____

_____

My Evaluation Checklist for a Speech

> **Evaluation Scale:**   1 = poor/none   3 = average   5 = excellent
> 2 = fair   4 = above average

▶ **Topic and Purpose**

_____ ■ Topic limited and manageable

_____ ■ Specific purpose established

▶ **Introduction**

_____ ■ Gets attention

_____ ■ Makes purpose clear

_____ ■ Gives needed information

_____ ■ Relates topic to audience

▶ **Development**

_____ ■ Main points clearly and logically organized

_____ ■ Effective transitions

_____ ■ Enough supporting evidence

_____ ■ Evidence is relevant to audience and purpose

_____ ■ Evidence clearly presented

▶ **Conclusion**

_____ ■ Emphasizes main points

_____ ■ Provides note of finality

_____ ■ Ends with high interest

▶ **Verbal Delivery**

_____ ■ Rate appropriate

_____ ■ Volume appropriate

_____ ■ Pronunciation correct

_____ ■ Enunciation clear

_____ ■ Stresses, emphasis appropriate

_____ ■ Pauses appropriate

_____ ■ Tone appropriate

▶ **Nonverbal Delivery**

_____ ■ Gestures appropriate

_____ ■ Facial expressions appropriate

_____ ■ Eye contact good

_____ ■ Posture acceptable

_____ ■ Other body language appropriate

_____ ■ Nervousness under control

▶ **Use of Visual and Audio Aids**

_____ ■ Microphone handled smoothly

_____ ■ All visual aids (videos, multimedia presentations, overhead transparencies, posters, slides) are clear and large enough for the audience to see

_____ ■ All audio aids (cassette tapes, CDs, etc.) are clearly audible to audience

_____ ■ All visual or audio aids enhance the presentation by clarifying a point or providing a memory aid for the audience; none are distracting or simply ornamental

▶ **Language**

_____ ■ Word choice appropriate

_____ ■ Level of formality/informality appropriate to occasion

My Evaluation of a Speech

Answer the following questions about a speech given by one of your classmates or one you heard outside of school.

Speaker _____ **Speech Topic**_____

- What was the speaker's purpose?

- How did the speaker's introduction get your attention?

- What main points did the speaker make?

- What evidence did the speaker give to support his or her points?

- Describe the speaker's verbal delivery. Was it effective? Why or why not?

- Describe the speaker's body language. Was it effective? Why or why not?

- Describe any visual or audio aids the speaker used. Were they effective? Why or why not?

- Was the tone of the speech appropriate for the audience, purpose, and occasion? Why or why not?

- What did you like best about this speech? Why?

- What suggestions would you give the speaker for how to improve the speech?

Evaluating My Oral Presentation of a Literary Text

Subject of the presentation _____

▶ Questions about my oral presentation of a literary text	▶ My responses
■ What criteria did I use to select the text (personal interest, universal appeal, interesting theme, exciting story, etc.)?	
■ Was my choice of text appropriate for my audience (subject matter, level of difficulty, length)? Why?	
■ After studying the text, what interpretation did I make? Was it valid or appropriate? Why?	
■ Did I prepare an introduction that provided information about the text, its author, and any important background information?	
■ Did I prepare a script of the text with cuts, notes for delivery, and marks for emphasis?	
■ Did I practice my presentation? ■ How did this help my delivery?	
■ How did I use verbal and nonverbal clues such as pitch, tone of voice, emphasis, posture, eye contact, facial expressions, and gestures to support my interpretation of the text?	
■ Did my verbal and nonverbal strategies fit my purpose, audience, and occasion? Why?	
■ How did I make sure that my delivery was clear and audible to everyone in my audience?	
■ What did I learn from this performance that can be used to improve my next presentation?	

My Evaluation of an Oral Presentation of a Literary Text

Speaker's name _____ **Subject of presentation** _____

Questions about the presentation	My responses
■ Was the literature appropriate to the audience and occasion?	
■ Did the speaker introduce the presentation with any background information or information about the author?	
■ How did the speaker use tone of voice, pitch, gestures, and facial expression to depict different characters?	
■ In what ways did the speaker use his or her own voice and tone to reflect the meaning and mood of the literary text?	
■ What vocal techniques did the speaker use to emphasize the rhyme or rhythm of the text? ■ How did these techniques help me to appreciate the artistic qualities of the text?	

Questions about my active listening	My responses
■ As I listened, did I try to predict what events or descriptions were coming next? ■ What clues enabled me to do this? ■ If I did not do this, how would predictions have helped my listening?	
■ Did I create mental images of events or descriptions as I listened? ■ If so, how did this increase my understanding or appreciation? ■ If not, how might this have helped my listening?	
■ What personal connections did I make with the text as the speaker spoke? ■ How did such connections help my understanding, especially of theme?	
■ Was I able to make eye contact with the speaker? ■ What nonverbal feedback did I give to the speaker?	

My Evaluation of Informative Oral Presentations

Speaker's name _____ **Type of message** _____

▶ Questions about the message	▶ My responses
■ Was the purpose of the message clear? ■ Why or why not?	
■ Did the message have an attention-getting introduction? ■ Why or why not?	
■ Did the message seem appropriate to the audience's interests and level of knowledge? ■ Why or why not?	
■ Were the main ideas or major steps easy to identify? Did they follow a logical pattern? ■ Why or why not?	
■ Were the key points of the message supported by sufficient details and reliable data? ■ Why do you think so?	
■ Did the message contain precise language? ■ Were words specific and concrete? ■ Was the vocabulary appropriate to the audience?	
■ Were visuals or sounds used to reinforce key points of the message? ■ If so, were they effective? How?	
■ Did the speaker seem confident? ■ Were the speaker's facial expressions, gestures, and movements natural?	
■ What suggestions do you have for improving the message or the speaker's delivery?	

NAME _____ CLASS _____ DATE _____

My Evaluation of Persuasive Oral Presentations

Speaker's name _____ **Subject of presentation** _____

▶ Questions about the message	▶ My responses
■ Did the introduction grab the audience's attention? ■ If so, how?	
■ Did the message seem appropriate to the interests, knowledge, and attitude of the audience? Explain.	
■ Did the speaker clearly state the specific purpose of the message? ■ What was it?	
■ Were reasons and supporting evidence clearly stated? ■ Did the evidence seem credible, or trustworthy? ■ Why or why not?	
■ Were ethical or emotional appeals used to motivate the audience? ■ Were they effective? Why or why not?	
■ Were opposing viewpoints presented and refuted with reasons and evidence? ■ If so, how?	
■ Did the message contain precise language? ■ Were words specific and concrete? ■ Was the vocabulary appropriate to the audience?	
■ Were visuals or sounds used to reinforce key points of the message? ■ If so, were they effective? How?	
■ Did the speaker seem confident and authoritative? ■ Were the speaker's facial expressions, gestures, and movements natural?	
■ What suggestions do you have for improving the message or the speaker's delivery?	

My Evaluation of Oral Storytelling

Ratings:

| 1 (poor) | 2 | 3 (average) | 4 | 5 (superior) |

EVALUATION CRITERIA	RATING	COMMENTS: Examples and explanations
■ The speaker chose a story that was interesting to the intended audience.		
■ The speaker provided background information that was useful in understanding or appreciating the story.		
■ The story was told in chronological order and events built upon one another in a suspenseful way.		
■ The storyteller used formal English, except when he or she was trying to depict certain characters.		
■ The storyteller used vivid verbs and descriptive language.		
■ The storyteller used the pitch and volume of his or her voice to convey mood and to depict certain characters.		
■ The storyteller used appropriate gestures and facial expressions.		
■ The storyteller combined words and gestures effectively.		
■ The storyteller didn't include long, wordy passages that could have been more effective if acted out with gestures.		
■ The story seemed well rehearsed and smooth.		

My Evaluation of a Panel Discussion

▶ **Ratings:**

1 (poor)	2	3 (average)	4	5 (superior)

▶ CRITERIA FOR EVALUATION	▶ RATING	▶ COMMENTS: Examples and explanations
Preparation ■ The issue to be discussed is clearly defined. ■ The participants' use of relevant details and evidence shows that they have analyzed the topic (and done research, if necessary) before the panel discussion.		
Participants' speaking skills and courtesy ■ Participants use an appropriate volume and tone of voice. ■ Participants do not interrupt one another. ■ Participants clearly and thoughtfully answer the questions of other participants, the moderator, and the audience.		
Participants' listening skills ■ Participants ask relevant questions, use appropriate body language, and make appropriate comments to show the speaker that they are listening. ■ Participants take notes when others are speaking. ■ Participants demonstrate that they have listened to others by commenting on or summarizing the preceding speaker's response before delivering their own responses.		
Moderator's role ■ The moderator introduces the discussion by providing essential information. ■ The moderator ensures that everyone has a chance to participate. ■ The moderator keeps the discussion on track. ■ The moderator keeps the question-and-answer session focused on brief questions and answers.		

My Evaluation of a Group Discussion

Ratings:

1 (poor)	2	3 (average)	4	5 (superior)

CRITERIA FOR EVALUATION	RATING	COMMENTS: Examples and explanations
Purpose ■ The group goal is clearly stated as a question to be answered or a problem to be solved. ■ Members of the group are prepared to explore the question or topic.		
Member Participation ■ Each member contributes information and opinions. ■ Each member asks relevant questions of other members. ■ Members stay on task. ■ Members maintain eye contact with other members and speak audibly and clearly.		
Courtesy ■ Members pay close attention to one another. ■ Members do not interrupt one another. ■ Members express any disagreements politely.		
Outcome ■ The group produces an answer to the original question or problem. ■ The majority of the group members agree with the group's conclusion.		

Overall evaluation

What was the strongest contribution to the discussion? Why?

What communication skills should the group continue to work on?

TEACHER'S REPORT

Progress in Speaking

▶ **Ratings:**

1 = minimal progress	4 = more progress than expected
2 = less progress than expected	5 = outstanding progress
3 = some progress	

▶ Speaking behaviors	▶ Rating	▶ Comments
Volunteers to recite in class or to contribute to class discussion		
Communicates effectively with classmates one-on-one		
Comments indicate keen audience awareness		
Contributions are on-topic and of interest		
Expresses self clearly and logically both in formal and informal speaking		
Uses details effectively when speaking		
Is developing effective control of voice		
Can be persuasive when talking		
Contributes orally to goals of smaller groups		

TEACHER'S REPORT

Progress in Listening

Ratings:	1 = minimal progress	4 = more progress than expected
	2 = less progress than expected	5 = outstanding progress
	3 = some progress	

Listening behaviors	**Rating**	**Comments**
Can follow orally presented instruction		
Pays attention to in-class contributions of classmates		
Responds in conversation in a way that indicates comprehension		
Participates in alternating exchange of ideas during conversation		
Follows orally administered directions appropriately		
Listens with a purpose; can ignore distractions		
Can adjust type of listening (critical, reflective, empathetic, or aesthetic) to suit purpose and occasion		
Is developing preferences for particular listening experiences (music, theater, etc.)		

TEACHER'S REPORT

Progress in Oral Presentation of Literary Texts

Ratings:

1 = minimal progress	4 = more progress than expected
2 = less progress than expected	5 = outstanding progress
3 = some progress	

Presentation criteria	Rating	Comments
Makes appropriate selections of texts		
Prepares script with cuts, marks for emphasis, and notes for delivery		
Prepares an informative and appropriate introduction of the text		
Practices presentation of oral interpretation		
Performs a valid interpretation of the text		
Uses verbal skills (pitch, tone of voice, emphasis) to communicate mood, meaning, and characterization		
Uses nonverbal skills (posture, eye contact, facial expressions, gestures) to communicate mood, meaning, and characterization		
Speaks clearly and audibly, with effective vocal variety		
Uses suggestions from others to improve personal performances		

Progress in Evaluation of Oral Presentations of Literary Texts

Ratings:	1 = minimal progress	4 = more progress than expected
	2 = less progress than expected	5 = outstanding progress
	3 = some progress	

Listening behaviors and perceptions	Rating	Comments
Listens to oral presentations actively		
Develops appreciation for spoken language		
Appreciates how nonverbal gestures and strategies enhance the spoken text		
Identifies the story line in narrative texts; makes predictions about what will come next		
Makes a personal connection with the literature; understands how this connection enhances his or her appreciation and understanding of literature		
Interprets themes; thinks about how oral performance reveals theme, mood, and characterization		
Recognizes and analyzes use of aesthetic language (figures of speech, imagery)		
Discusses how use of aesthetic language enhances literary texts		

TEACHER'S REPORT

Progress in Evaluating Oral Presentations of Informative and Persuasive Messages

Ratings:

1 = minimal progress	4 = more progress than expected
2 = less progress than expected	5 = outstanding progress
3 = some progress	

Listening behaviors	Rating	Comments
Examines the organizational structure of the message		
Evaluates the support offered for the key points in the message		
Examines the use of visual and audio aids in the message		
Evaluates the effectiveness of the language used in the message, including the precision of explanations and/or the use of emotional appeals and other persuasive techniques		
Evaluates the comprehensiveness and fairness of the message		
Identifies strengths and weaknesses in the delivery of the message		
Evaluates the impact of message on the intended audience		

TEACHER'S REPORT

Progress in Evaluating Oral Storytelling

Ratings:

1 = minimal progress
2 = less progress than expected
3 = some progress

4 = more progress than expected
5 = outstanding progress

Behaviors and perceptions	Rating	Comments
Evaluates whether story will interest audience		
Evaluates whether background information is necessary, and, if given, whether it is adequate		
Evaluates order of story's presentation and determines whether it is effective, clear, and suspenseful		
Evaluates the effectiveness of the storyteller's language, including the vividness of the descriptions and action verbs		
Evaluates how effectively the storyteller uses his or her voice to convey characterization and mood		
Evaluates storyteller's gestures and facial expressions for appropriateness and helpfulness in telling the story		
Identifies sections in the story where description might have been cut in favor of gesture and vice versa		
Evaluates the smoothness of the storyteller's presentation		

Progress in Evaluating Panel Discussions

Ratings:
1 = minimal progress
2 = less progress than expected
3 = some progress

4 = more progress than expected
5 = outstanding progress

Behaviors and perceptions	Rating	Comments
Identifies the topic to be discussed		
Evaluates participants' preparation for the panel discussion; notes whether they have obviously analyzed the topic or done research		
Evaluates participants' volume and tone of voice for clarity and appropriateness		
Evaluates participants' courtesy		
Evaluates participants' attentiveness to other speakers as shown by note taking, body language, questions, and comments		
Evaluates the moderator's effectiveness in ensuring that everyone has a chance to participate		
Evaluates the moderator's success in keeping the discussion on track		

TEACHER'S REPORT

Progress in Evaluating Group Discussions

Ratings:

1 = minimal progress	4 = more progress than expected
2 = less progress than expected	5 = outstanding progress
3 = some progress	

Behaviors and perceptions	Rating	Comments
Identifies the group goal		
Evaluates whether members are prepared to explore the topic or question		
Evaluates how well the group seems to stay on task		
Evaluates members' contributions to the discussion; notes whether each member contributes information and asks relevant questions of other members		
Evaluates whether members are engaged with the group; notes whether members maintain eye contact with one another and whether they speak audibly and clearly		
Evaluates members' courtesy towards one another		
Assesses whether the group reaches its goal		
Assesses whether the majority of the members agree with the group's conclusion		

My Viewing Record

Use this record for different types of television programs, Web sites, films, and videos. Log at least one viewing experience per week.

> ▶ **Ratings:** ✓✓✓✓ This was very important! ✓✓ I learned a little.
> ✓✓✓ Worth doing/remembering ✓ I wasted my time.

Date:

What I saw:

Notes about why this experience was or was not important, interesting, or useful:

Rating:

Date:

What I saw:

Notes about why this experience was or was not important, interesting, or useful:

Rating:

Date:

What I saw:

Notes about why this experience was or was not important, interesting, or useful:

Rating:

Inventory: Some Questions and Answers About My Viewing

▶ Questions and answers about my viewing	▶ More about my answers
What kinds of visual media do I use or prefer—television, film, Web, or another type?	What do I like about these kinds of media?
What kinds of television shows and movies do I prefer?	Why do I like them the best?
How much am I influenced by what I see? For example, how apt am I to purchase something I have seen advertised?	What associations do I make between the image I see and myself? What emotions do I think advertising plays on?
Who makes the TV shows, magazines, or videos I like best?	What do I think is the purpose of these programs, magazines, or videos?
Who is the target audience of the shows and other media I like? How do I know?	How would people outside this target audience interpret these shows or other media?
Do I evaluate visual or audio techniques (close shots, objects out of focus, music, voice-overs, etc.)?	How aware of these techniques am I as I watch?

Inventory: Some Questions and Answers About My Representing

Questions and answers about my representing	More about my answers
What visual media do I like to use—videos, Web, painting, drawing, or another form?	What do I like about using these visual media?
Before beginning any project, do I think about which visual medium would best suit my purpose?	How do visual media differ? What are their individual strengths and weaknesses?
Do I continually consider my audience when creating visual media?	How do my final products show that I've thought about audience?
Do I consider design elements such as color, line, graphics, images, and photos when using visual media?	How and why do I use design elements?
Do I think about how a viewer or reader will navigate through the visual media I make—particularly Web sites?	How do I make sure that my information is complete without being cluttered or disorganized?
When using film or video, do I consider how the sound and picture will work together?	How do I make sure that the sound and images in my film or video complement each other?

My Evaluation of Multimedia Presentations

▶ **Ratings:**

| 1 (poor) | 2 | 3 (average) | 4 | 5 (superior) |

CRITERIA FOR EVALUATION	RATING	COMMENTS: Examples and explanations
Content ■ The presenter states the purpose of the presentation at the beginning. ■ The presentation is interesting and informative. ■ The presentation is organized in an effective way.		
Delivery ■ The presenter speaks clearly and loudly enough to be heard by the entire audience. ■ The speaker gives the audience enough time to look at each visual. ■ The speaker faces the audience during most of the presentation, only looking away when pointing out something on the computer or video screen. ■ The speaker operates all equipment smoothly.		
Visuals ■ The visuals present essential and relevant information. ■ The speaker presents the visuals at the same time as the points they reinforce. ■ Charts, graphs, and photos are easy to read and understand. ■ Charts and graphs use color or design elements to make the information clearer.		
Music/sound effects ■ The music sets a mood. ■ The sound effects match the images. ■ The music or sound effects are not distracting.		

My Evaluation of a Documentary

DIRECTIONS: Circle the number in each row below to indicate your evaluation of each item.

Ratings:	1 = Poorly done	4 = Good
	2 = Has some flaws	5 = Superior
	3 = Average	

I. CONTENT

The documentary reveals a main idea.	1 2 3 4 5
The documentary is interesting.	1 2 3 4 5
The documentary contributes to the viewer's understanding of the topic.	1 2 3 4 5
The documentary provides a variety of content—images of the narrator, interviews, action sequences, graphs, still photos, and so on.	1 2 3 4 5
The documentary presents its subject accurately and fairly.	1 2 3 4 5

II. ORGANIZATION

The beginning of the documentary introduces the subject and grabs your attention.	1 2 3 4 5
Each scene gives new information.	1 2 3 4 5
The sequence of scenes makes sense; if appropriate, the sequence of shots builds suspense.	1 2 3 4 5
The voice-over fits with the action and dialogue.	1 2 3 4 5
The end of the documentary sums up the information presented and leaves you with a final impression.	1 2 3 4 5

III. TECHNICAL QUALITY

The sound quality is audible and consistent.	1 2 3 4 5
The music adds atmosphere without distracting from the action or dialogue.	1 2 3 4 5
The camera angles are clear and interesting.	1 2 3 4 5
The combination of camera shots is smooth; transitions are used effectively between shots.	1 2 3 4 5
Lighting is used to enhance atmosphere.	1 2 3 4 5

Overall Evaluation or Comments:

My Evaluation of a Newspaper

Choose a school, local, or national newspaper and answer the following questions.

1. Who is the intended audience for the newspaper? Why do you think so?

2. Is there a mix of stories and features in the paper, including hard-hitting news stories, human interest stories, editorials, and so on? What kinds of stories take up the most space?

3. How well organized is the layout? Are photos mixed in with the text? Are story headlines presented and arranged in an appealing way?

4. What kind of visuals are used? What purpose do they seem to have?

5. Choose a particular story on the front page, and state the story's main idea.

6. In the particular story you chose, look for quotations. Why are these people's words used in the story?

7. Ask yourself how the *5W-How?* questions (*who? what? where? when? why?* and *how?*) are answered in the story. If these questions aren't answered, why not?

8. Do you think the newspaper is informative and fair? Why or why not?

My Evaluation of a Photograph

Choose a photograph from a newspaper story and answer the following questions.

1. Describe what the photo portrays.

2. From what camera angle is the photo taken—from above, below, or some other angle?

3. Explain the effect of the camera angle on your response to the photo. Does it make the subject look fragile, intimidating, or something else?

4. How is the photo cropped? What do you suspect might be just outside the frame of the photo?

5. Would you react differently to the photo if you could see more of the scene or if the photo was a tighter close-up? Explain your answer.

6. Does the photo's caption give you just factual information, or does it show a positive or negative view of the photo? Explain your answer.

7. What other caption could you give the photo? How might that caption change how viewers respond to the photo?

8. How does the photo make you feel? Does it invite an emotional reaction? Explain.

9. How does the photo contribute to the text of the story? Does it convey important information?

My Evaluation of a Television News Program

View a news program and take notes. Then, answer the following questions.

1. Name the news program you are evaluating. Is it a national news program, a local news program, or a newsmagazine? Who do you think is its primary audience?

2. Name some of the stories presented and then explain why you think they were shown. Did they meet the common news criteria of timeliness, serious impact on the audience, human interest, or news about celebrities?

3. Choose a particular news story and explain how it captures the viewer's attention. Do its words or images play upon the viewer's emotions? If so, how?

4. Whose points of view are represented in the story? Whose are left out? Why?

5. Who reports the news? Do reporters in the field and outside experts interact with the anchors or not? Why do you think this is (or is not) done?

6. What do the program's set, slogan, title logo, and opening music tell you about its tone and purpose?

7. What advertisements are shown in the commercials that interrupt the show? Why do you think they are the ones used?

8. How reliable do you think this news program is? Why do you think so?

My Comparison of Media: Film and Literature

Use this form to evaluate and compare a story or book and its TV or film version.

1. What are the names of the story or book and the TV or film adaptation of the story?

2. What genre do the story or book and its adaptation belong to—science fiction, animal stories, mysteries, Westerns, or another genre? What are the characteristics of this genre?

3. How does the TV or film version represent the plot of the story or book? Does it add events or leave them out? Why?

4. How does the TV or film version depict the main characters of the book? If there are significant changes, what are they and why do you think they were made?

5. How well does the TV or film version use dialogue to tell the story or convey the emotions of the characters? Is the dialogue faithful to the book or story? Why or why not?

6. How do the actors in the TV or film version use facial expressions and body movements to convey what the characters feel?

7. What camera techniques (close-ups, long shots) does the film use to tell the story or convey the characters' emotions? Are they effective?

8. What is your overall evaluation of the TV or film version of the book or story? How does it compare to the printed text? Explain your answer.

My Evaluation of a Television Entertainment Program

View a television sitcom or drama and take notes. Then, answer the following questions.

1. What is the name of the show?

2. What is the show's genre—drama, sitcom, or some other type of program? What are the characteristics of that type of program?

3. What audience do you think it targets? Why do you think so?

4. What is the main plot of the show? Is it realistic? Why or why not?

5. What is the main setting of the show? Is it realistic? Why or why not?

6. Who are the main characters on the show? Are they realistic, or "round," characters—or are they stereotypes? What makes you think so?

7. How do you respond to the characters? Do you identify with them? Why or why not?

8. What is the theme of the show? Why do you think so?

9. What is your overall assessment of the show? Why?

My Evaluation of Graphics

DIRECTIONS: Circle a number in each row below to indicate your evaluation of each item.

> **Ratings:** 1 = Poorly done   4 = Good
>   2 = Has some flaws   5 = Superior
>   3 = Average

I. PLANNING

- The graphic is an appropriate way to communicate the information. 1 2 3 4 5

- The graphic gives enough information to make the process or results clearly 1 2 3 4 5
  understandable, but not so much information that the graphic is cluttered or
  distracting.

- The graphic supports a point made in the essay, article, or presentation. 1 2 3 4 5

II. LABELS

- The graphic has a clear title or caption. 1 2 3 4 5

- Labels are accurate and complete but not wordy. 1 2 3 4 5

- The graphic has a clear key or legend. 1 2 3 4 5

- If the information represented was found in a research source, the source is 1 2 3 4 5
  clearly identified.

III. DESIGN AND SPATIAL ORGANIZATION

- If color is used, it is limited to just a few colors that are used consistently. 1 2 3 4 5

- The movement in a flowchart is clear; arrows direct the reader's eye in a 1 2 3 4 5
  logical pattern.

- The vertical and horizontal axes of a bar or line graph are clearly identified, 1 2 3 4 5
  so the reader can tell what is being measured and what measurements are
  being used.

- The wedges of a pie chart are labeled and arranged in a logical way. 1 2 3 4 5

- Charts and tables have easily identifiable categories listed at the top. 1 2 3 4 5

- Time lines clearly show events from left to right. 1 2 3 4 5

Overall Evaluation:

My Evaluation of a Television Commercial

Use this form to evaluate a television commercial. If possible, tape the commercial so you can watch it a number of times during your evaluation.

1. What is the product or service being advertised?

2. Who made the ad and why?

3. Who is the target audience of the ad? Why do you think so?

4. Describe who or what is featured in the ad. Why are these people or things shown?

5. What is the setting of the ad? Why is this setting used?

6. Do you detect any persuasive techniques, such as bandwagon, snob appeal, and so on? Why are they effective (or ineffective)?

7. Does the ad have a plot or story? If so, how does it contribute to the ad's message?

8. How does music or sound contribute to the ad's message or appeal to the target audience?

9. How do camera angles contribute to the ad's message or appeal to the ad's target audience?

10. Does the ad appeal to your emotions, logic, or ethics? If so, how and why?

11. What show were you watching when you saw the ad? What does that show tell you about the purpose and target audience of the ad?

12. Is the ad effective? Why or why not?

My Evaluation of a Print Advertisement

Use this form to evaluate an advertisement from a newspaper or magazine.

1. What is the message of the ad?

2. Who made the ad and why?

3. Who is the target audience of the ad? Why do you think so?

4. Does the ad appeal to the reader's intellect by presenting valid, logical reasons? If so, what are they?

5. Does the ad use persuasive techniques (bandwagon, testimonial, plain folks, loaded words, and so on) to appeal to the reader's emotions and desires? What techniques does it use and why are they effective (or ineffective)?

6. Does the ad use images to effectively appeal to the reader's emotions or senses? What are they? Why are they effective (or ineffective)?

7. How does the ad use color, line, shape, texture, or camera angle to catch the reader's attention and reinforce the message?

8. Does the ad have a catchy slogan? Is the slogan appropriate for the target audience? Explain.

9. Does the ad accurately represent its product, service, idea, or cause? Why or why not?

10. How effective is the ad? Why?

My Evaluation of a Web Site

Ratings:

| 1 (poor) | 2 | 3 (average) | 4 | 5 (superior) |

CRITERIA FOR EVALUATION	RATING	COMMENTS: Examples and explanations
Clarity ■ The site is easy to navigate. ■ The site contains a clear index. ■ Hyperlinks are clearly distinguished from text. ■ Text is easy to read.		
Content ■ The site contains complete information. ■ The site is objective or makes an effort to present both sides of an issue. ■ The site's producer is clearly identified on the home page. ■ The site is authoritative; the site and its producer seem to be trustworthy sources of information. ■ The content is current; the last revision date on the page is reasonably recent.		
Design ■ Color is used effectively—one color is used consistently for each different element of the site (hyperlinks, headings, etc.). ■ Photos, graphics, or animation enhance the site without distracting the viewer. ■ Visuals download quickly.		
Organization ■ All closely related information is located on a single page. ■ The pages are not crowded with too much text. ■ The information is organized in a logical way.		

Progress in Viewing

Ratings:

1 = minimal progress	4 = more progress than expected
2 = less progress than expected	5 = outstanding progress
3 = some progress	

Viewing perceptions and behaviors	Rating	Comments
Identifies the purpose of various media presentations (i.e., informative, advertising, entertainment shows)		
Analyzes credibility of programs viewed (who made it and why)		
Speculates about the target audience of a media message and identifies what techniques are used to address that audience		
Analyzes own response to different kinds of media messages		
Evaluates audio and visual techniques (special effects, camera angles, music, etc.) and their effects		
Draws conclusions and forms opinions about the purpose and effects of media messages		
Articulates reasons for personal preferences in TV and movie viewing		

TEACHER'S REPORT

Progress in Representing

Ratings:

1 = minimal progress   4 = more progress than expected

2 = less progress than expected   5 = outstanding progress

3 = some progress

Representing behaviors and perceptions	Rating	Comments
Chooses medium appropriate to his or her purpose		
Considers target audience and how to attract its members		
Provides accurate, complete information without disorganization or clutter		
Uses color, line, graphics, images, and photos to attract attention and provide clear information		
Considers how a viewer or reader will navigate through the media product; the design of product reflects thinking about the ease of its use		
If the product is a film or video, uses sound and images to complement each other; product reflects student's awareness of effective expository or storytelling techniques		
Reflects on the strengths and weaknesses of the final product		

TEACHER'S REPORT

Progress in Evaluating Multimedia Presentations

Ratings:
- 1 = minimal progress
- 2 = less progress than expected
- 3 = some progress
- 4 = more progress than expected
- 5 = outstanding progress

Behaviors and perceptions	Rating	Comments
Identifies the purpose of the presentation		
Evaluates whether the presentation is informative and interesting		
Evaluates how well the visuals support the purpose of the presentation; can detect whether they are irrelevant or used solely for ornamentation		
Evaluates the clarity of the visuals		
Evaluates the organization of the presentation		
Evaluates the effectiveness and relevance of the music and/or sound effects		
Evaluates the presenter's delivery		

TEACHER'S REPORT

Progress in Evaluating Documentaries

Ratings:	1 = minimal progress	4 = more progress than expected
	2 = less progress than expected	5 = outstanding progress
	3 = some progress	

Behaviors and perceptions	Rating	Comments
Identifies the topic and overall purpose of the documentary		
Evaluates the documentary's camera work and editing; identifies the purpose or intended effect of certain shots and edits		
Evaluates the documentary's use of music and sound effects; assesses how well sound and image complement each other		
Evaluates the documentary's organization; assesses whether the sequences and transitions make sense and create interest		
Evaluates the documentary's use of lighting to create mood and to portray scenes clearly		
Evaluates the documentary's point of view and fairness		
Evaluates the documentary's thoroughness; can cite details that reveal the maker's knowledge and/or research		
Assesses the informativeness and entertainment value of the documentary		

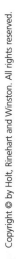

Progress in Evaluating Newspapers

Ratings:
1 = minimal progress
2 = less progress than expected
3 = some progress
4 = more progress than expected
5 = outstanding progress

Behaviors and perceptions	Rating	Comments
Speculates about the newspaper's intended audience		
Evaluates the mix of stories in the paper and identifies which type of stories are most prominent		
Evaluates the design of the paper, including layout, fonts, and placement of text and images		
Evaluates visuals and their effects and purposes		
Can identify emotional appeals and shows awareness of why they are used in stories and photos		
Identifies quotations in a particular story and evaluates whether they are from appropriate and authoritative sources		
Can evaluate whether a particular news story answers the *5W-H?* questions and, if not, can speculate about why not		

TEACHER'S REPORT

Progress in Evaluating Photographs

Ratings:

1 = minimal progress
2 = less progress than expected
3 = some progress

4 = more progress than expected
5 = outstanding progress

Behaviors and perceptions	Rating	Comments
Can describe photo in detail		
Can identify the angle from which the photo is taken and what effect that angle has on the viewer's response		
Can tell how photo is cropped or speculate about what lies outside the photo's frame		
Can assess the effect of cropping on the viewer's response to the photo		
Can evaluate the tone and purpose of the caption		
Can identify how the caption affects the viewer's response to the photo		
Can assess how the photo makes him or her feel about the subject of the photo		
Can assess how the photo contributes to the text of the news story		
Can assess the photo's effectiveness in conveying information		
Can give specific and relevant reasons for his or her answers		

TEACHER'S REPORT

Progress in Evaluating Television News

▶ **Ratings:**

1 = minimal progress	4 = more progress than expected
2 = less progress than expected	5 = outstanding progress
3 = some progress	

▶ Behaviors and perceptions	▶ Rating	▶ Comments
Can identify the genre of the news program and identify some of its characteristics		
Can identify the criteria the news program's producers might have used in choosing individual stories		
Can speculate about target audience and offer support for his or her ideas		
Evaluates fairness of stories; notes whose point of view is adopted and whose is omitted		
Evaluates visuals and their possible emotional impact		
Assesses the show's anchors, set, slogan, and music; notes how all elements contribute to the purpose and tone of the show		
Assesses what information the interrupting advertisements can provide about the audience and purpose of the show		
Evaluates the overall reliability of the show and provides support for opinion		

Progress in Evaluating Film and TV Entertainment Genres

Ratings:	1 = minimal progress	4 = more progress than expected
	2 = less progress than expected	5 = outstanding progress
	3 = some progress	

Behaviors and perceptions	Rating	Comments
Student identifies genre of show or film and can recall several characteristics of that genre		
Can thoughtfully speculate about target audience		
Evaluates setting		
Evaluates characters and dialogue; can distinguish complex characterization from stereotypes		
Evaluates plot		
Identifies theme and can provide support for answer		
If film or show is an adaptation of a literary work, can evaluate how well the actors, script, setting, and camera techniques capture the style and meaning of the text		
If film or show is an adaptation of a literary work, can speculate about why any changes in character, plot, or setting were made		
Can offer an overall assessment and provide support for this opinion		

Progress in Evaluating Graphics

Ratings: 1 = minimal progress   4 = more progress than expected
             2 = less progress than expected 5 = outstanding progress
             3 = some progress

Behaviors and perceptions	Rating	Comments
Evaluates the suitability of the graphic to convey the information it contains and the graphic's relevance to the text it supports		
Evaluates the completeness and clarity of the graphic; checks that the graphic is not cluttered with too much information		
Evaluates the completeness and clarity of the graphic's labels		
Identifies the graphic's key or legend and evaluates its clarity		
Evaluates the use of color for helpfulness and consistency		
Evaluates the logic and organization of charts, tables, flowcharts, graphs, and time lines		
Can support evaluations with clear reasons		

Progress in Evaluating Advertising

Ratings:

1 = minimal progress	4 = more progress than expected
2 = less progress than expected	5 = outstanding progress
3 = some progress	

Behaviors and perceptions	Rating	Comments
Identifies the purpose and target audience of the ad		
Evaluates the ad's slogan, written copy, voice-over, dialogue, or music for clarity, interest, and appropriateness for the target audience		
Identifies logical or ethical appeals in the ad		
Identifies persuasive techniques and emotional appeals and evaluates their effects		
Evaluates the ad's selection of images and use of color, line, texture, and camera angles		
Evaluates a television ad's use of characters and plot and speculates about the intended purpose and effect of these elements		
Evaluates the fairness of the ad		
Provides thoughtful reasons and concrete evidence for all evaluations		

Progress in Evaluating Web Sites

Ratings:	1 = minimal progress	4 = more progress than expected
	2 = less progress than expected	5 = outstanding progress
	3 = some progress	

Behaviors and perceptions	Rating	Comments
Evaluates the site's ease of navigation and the logic of its organization		
Evaluates the accuracy and objectivity of the site's information		
Identifies the site's producer and assesses his or her credibility		
Evaluates whether the site is current		
Evaluates the site's use of images, graphics, photos, and animation		
Evaluates the site's use of color for consistency and helpfulness		
Evaluates the site's overall design for clarity and absence of clutter		

My Cooperative Learning Record

Use this record to track and evaluate your conferences with peer partners, your discussions in small groups, your group projects, and your teacher conferences.

▶ **Ratings:** ✓✓✓✓ This was very important!   ✓✓ I learned a little.
              ✓✓✓ Worth doing/remembering   ✓ I wasted my time.

Date:

What I said, heard, or learned:

Notes about why this experience was or was not important, interesting, or useful:

Rating:

Date:

What I said, heard, or learned:

Notes about why this experience was or was not important, interesting, or useful:

Rating:

Date:

What I said, heard, or learned:

Notes about why this experience was or was not important, interesting, or useful:

Rating:

Inventory: Some Questions and Answers About My Cooperative Learning

▶ Questions and answers about cooperative learning	▶ More about my answers
How do I feel about my role in the group?	What do I feel this way?
How much responsibility do I assume?	Do I like doing this? Why or why not?
How much do I participate in the group?	What do others learn from me?
How well do I stay on task?	What do I learn from others?
What is the most difficult thing about cooperative learning?	Why is it difficult?
What do I like about working cooperatively with others?	How might I use cooperative learning skills outside of school?

Evaluation of My Cooperative Learning

Use these questions to consider and evaluate your contributions to group activities.

1. What was your role in the group?

_____

2. What did you need to do to be useful in that role?

_____

_____

_____

_____

3. Were you attentive and respectful to others in the group? What did you do to show these things?

_____

_____

_____

_____

4. Were you able to stick to the subject or project at hand? Why or why not?

_____

_____

_____

_____

5. What was your most important contribution to the group?

_____

_____

_____

_____

6. What could you do to become a more effective group member?

_____

_____

_____

NAME _____   CLASS _____   DATE _____

My Evaluation of Cooperative Learning

Use these questions to evaluate the contributions of another student in your group.

Group member's name: _____   **Group member's role in the group:** _____

1. Three words I would use to describe how the group member performed the role are
_____

2. The member did the following things to work well with others (for example, asked questions to clarify the task, organized the agenda, or showed courtesy to other members):

_____

_____

_____

_____

_____

3. The most important contribution the member made to the group was _____

_____

_____

_____

_____

4. This contribution was important to the group because _____

_____

_____

_____

_____

5. The group member could contribute more to the group if he or she _____

_____

_____

_____

Copyright © by Holt, Rinehart and Winston. All rights reserved.

142   ELEMENTS OF LANGUAGE | Introductory Course | *Assessment Alternatives*

PEER AND SELF-EVALUATION

My Evaluation of Group Participation

Think about the work your small group did and then answer the following questions.

1. The students who participated in this group were _____

_____

_____

2. Our task was _____

_____

_____

_____

3. ▶ Circle your response to the following statements.

   1 = Strongly Disagree   2 = Disagree Somewhat   3 = Agree   4 = Strongly Agree

The group did a good job of staying on task.	1	2	3	4
Every member of the group contributed to the group.	1	2	3	4
Each member of the group treated the other members of the group with respect and kindness.	1	2	3	4
The group felt that the task was worth accomplishing.	1	2	3	4
Each member of the group learned something from this experience.	1	2	3	4

4. What is the group's greatest strength? _____

_____

_____

_____

_____

_____

5. What does this group need to do to become more productive? _____

_____

_____

_____

_____

_____

Progress in Cooperative Learning

> **Ratings:**
>
> 1 = minimal progress   4 = more progress than expected
> 2 = less progress than expected   5 = outstanding progress
> 3 = some progress

Behaviors and perceptions	Rating	Comments
Actively participates in assigned role		
Communicates effectively with the group		
Assumes individual responsibility in learning		
Organizes work		
Focuses effectively on topic		
Demonstrates multiple problem-solving strategies		
Respects opinions, strengths, and weaknesses of others in group		
Demonstrates a positive attitude with the group		
Encourages others to participate		
Explains concepts; paraphrases and summarizes ideas		
Adds ideas and offers input		
Completes work		

Holistic Scale: Six Points

Score: 6 | **A score "6" paper has the following characteristics.**
All parts of the prompt are addressed with insight and control, and the writing is focused, clear, and well developed. All support is ample, specific, and relevant. The paper's organizational pattern enables a logical, coherent progression of ideas. The writer's engagement with the topic is clearly evident, as is his or her consideration of the intended audience. The writer makes controlled and effective word choices and uses a natural, fresh voice; the paper is free of clichés and wooden phrasing. Sentence structure is varied, and fragments are used only when appropriate to the writer's purpose. There are very few, if any, convention errors in mechanics, usage, and punctuation.

Score: 5 | **A score "5" paper has the following characteristics.**
The paper addresses all parts of the prompt with some degree of clarity and insight, although some minor lapses in coherence may be evident. The writer shows a consideration of purpose and audience, and the paper's organizational pattern is clear. All support is sufficient, specific, and relevant. When causal relationships are discussed, the writer makes all connections clear and explicit. The paper also exhibits a good command of language, including accurate and descriptive word choices. Sentence structure is varied, and sentences are complete except when fragments are used for effect. The writer makes few errors in mechanics, usage, and spelling.

Score: 4 | **A score "4" paper has the following characteristics.**
For the most part, the paper is focused on the topic but may include irrelevant or loosely related material. The writer uses an appropriate organizational pattern, although some confusion in the logical progression of ideas may occur. The support includes specific details and precise word choices but is not ample nor evenly elaborated. In some responses, the writer demonstrates an awareness of audience, although this awareness is not exhibited consistently throughout the paper. Most sentences are complete, but there is little variation in sentence structure. There are few egregious errors in grammar, usage, and spelling.

Score: 3 | **A score "3" paper has the following characteristics.**
The paper addresses the topic in a reasonably focused way but may include irrelevant or loosely related material. The writer attempts to follow an organizational pattern, but may lapse into digressions or fail to provide transitions between ideas. The paper may also demonstrate little awareness of or connection to an audience. Some support, which may include specific

Holistic Scale: Six Points *(continued)*

details and relevant examples, is included, but development of such support is not consistent or substantial. Some "3" papers may appear to be somewhat elaborated summaries or lists of ideas. The writer's choice of words is generally adequate, but may be predictable or imprecise. The writer may vary his or her sentence structure very little, or not at all. Usually, however, the writer has a command of the conventions of written language.

Score: 2

A score "2" paper has the following characteristics.

The paper is generally responsive to the prompt but includes irrelevant or loosely related material. The paper may show few signs of an overall organizational strategy and few explicit transitions between ideas. Some papers may not exhibit a logical relationship between the main idea and subordinate ideas. Others may have an initial sense of purpose but then veer off-track. Support is generally unelaborated, consisting of lists or simple summary. The writer's choice of words is often imprecise or inappropriate, and sentence structure is unvaried or faulty. The writer may show limited knowledge of the basic conventions of writing.

Score: 1

A score "1" paper has the following characteristics.

The paper may address the prompt in only a minimal or tangential way. In addition, the paper may be highly fragmentary, often a listing of ideas with little development of support. If any attempt to support or organize ideas is exhibited, a "1" paper is too short or skeletal to achieve a higher score. There is often no sense of audience or audience is badly misperceived. Inappropriate word choice or frequent errors in sentence structure may also completely hinder the paper's readability. The writer may make blatant errors in grammar, mechanics, and usage.

Unscorable

The paper is unscorable because
- the response is not relevant to the prompt.
- the response is only a rewording of the prompt.
- the response contains an insufficient amount of writing to determine if it addresses the prompt.
- the response is a copy of a previously published work.
- the response is illegible, incomprehensible, or blank.

Holistic Scale: Six Points

Score: 6

A score "6" paper has the following characteristics.

All parts of the prompt are addressed with insight and control, and the writing is focused, well developed, and forceful. The writer presents a clear recommendation based on thoughtful criteria. All support is specific, relevant, and persuasive. The paper's organizational pattern enables a logical progression of ideas. The paper also demonstrates the writer's engagement with the issue and his or her consideration of the audience. The writer makes controlled and effective word choices and reveals a natural, fresh voice. Sentence structure is varied and there are very few, if any, convention errors in mechanics, usage, and grammar. The response is written in a conventional letter format.

Score: 5

A score "5" paper has the following characteristics.

The paper addresses all parts of the prompt with insight, although some minor lapses in coherence may be evident. The writer shows that he or she understands the criteria that might be applied to a book, including literary concepts, and has considered audience. The paper's organizational pattern is clear and all support is sufficient, specific, relevant, and persuasive. The paper also exhibits a good command of language, including precise, forceful, and vivid word choices. Sentence structure is varied and the writer makes few errors in mechanics, usage, and grammar. Letter format is used, although it may not match a conventional format.

Score: 4

A score "4" paper has the following characteristics.

For the most part, the paper is focused on the evaluative task but may include some irrelevant or loosely related material. The writer uses an appropriate organizational pattern, although there may be occasional lapses in logic or coherence. The paper's support includes specific details, relevant examples, and precise word choices but is not ample nor evenly elaborated. In some responses, the writer demonstrates an awareness of audience, although this awareness may not be exhibited consistently throughout the paper. Most sentences are complete, but there is little variation in sentence structure. There are few egregious errors in mechanics, usage, and spelling. Letter format may be missing except for a greeting and/or closing.

Score: 3

A score "3" paper has the following characteristics.

The paper addresses the evaluative task in a reasonably focused way but may include irrelevant or loosely related material. The writer attempts to follow an organizational pattern, but may lapse into digressions or fail to provide

Holistic Scale: Six Points *(continued)*

transitions between ideas. The paper may also demonstrate little awareness of audience. Some support is included, but elaboration is not consistent or substantial. The writer's choice of words is generally adequate, but may be predictable or imprecise. The writer may also vary his or her sentence structure very little, or not at all. Usually, however, the writer has a command of the basic conventions of writing. Letter format and paragraphing may be missing.

Score: 2

A score "2" paper has the following characteristics.
The paper is generally responsive to the prompt but includes irrelevant or loosely related material. Many "2" papers will not offer a clear opinion about the book nor cite criteria for judgment. The paper may show few signs of an overall organizational strategy and few clear transitions between ideas. Some papers may have an initial sense of purpose but then veer off-track. Support is generally unelaborated, consisting of lists or simple summary. The writer's choice of words is often imprecise or inappropriate, and sentence structure is not adequately varied. The writer may show limited knowledge of the basic conventions of writing. No attempt at letter format is made.

Score: 1

A score "1" paper has the following characteristics.
The paper may address the prompt in only a minimal or tangential way. In addition, the paper may be highly fragmentary, often a listing of ideas with little development of support. Frequently, no organizational pattern is apparent. If any attempt to support or organize ideas is exhibited, a "1" paper is too short or skeletal to achieve a higher score. There is often no sense of audience. Inappropriate word choice or frequent errors in sentence structure may also completely hinder the paper's readability. The writer may make blatant errors in grammar, mechanics, and usage. The writer does not use a letter format or paragraphing.

Unscorable

The paper is unscorable because
- the response is not relevant to the prompt.
- the response is only a rewording of the prompt.
- the response contains an insufficient amount of writing to determine if it addresses the prompt.
- the response is a copy of a previously published work.
- the response is illegible, incomprehensible, or blank.

Holistic Scale: Four Points

Score Point 4

Responses that are organized, elaborated, and highly readable attempts to clarify, explain, or present information about the specified topic. Although a score "4" paper may exhibit a few inconsistencies, such inconsistencies are eclipsed by the overall quality, coherence, and thoughtfulness of the response.

- *The most characteristic trait of these responses is the ample and relevant support they contain; all ideas are specific and well-elaborated. Such responses are also characterized by most of the following:*

  ✓ *A unified organizational plan.* The responses have a clear organization and seem complete; if the writer employs more than one organizational strategy, all ideas still follow a logical progression. Minor inconsistencies may occur, but they do not detract from the overall order of the paper. In cases in which writers have run out of space, especially well-organized papers may still receive a "4."

  ✓ *A marked command of written language.* These responses are fluent and clear; although some writers may not use all of the appropriate conventions of language, these responses are nevertheless quite skillfully written.

  ✓ *Varied syntactic construction.* These responses contain compound and complex sentences.

  ✓ *Concrete, vivid details.* All descriptions and explanations are communicated through thoughtful and effective word choices and expressions.

  ✓ *Attention to all parts of the prompt.*

Score Point 3

Responses that are good efforts to clarify, explain, or present information about the specified topic. For the most part, a reader finds the paper clear, coherent, and reasonably elaborated.

- *The "3" category is composed of the following kinds of responses:*

  ✓ *Papers that offer a great number of ideas, one of which is moderately elaborated, several of which are somewhat elaborated, or most of which are extended.*

  ✓ *Papers that offer many ideas, most of which are somewhat elaborated.*

  ✓ *Papers that offer two or more moderately elaborated ideas.*

- *These papers have the following characteristics:*

  ✓ *A reasonably consistent organizational plan.* Occasional inconsistencies may be evident. Responses may also include extraneous or loosely related material.

  ✓ *Control of written language.* Some errors in spelling, capitalization, punctuation, and/or usage may appear, but they do not unduly distract the reader.

  ✓ *A clear understanding of the topic, although all parts of the prompt may not be addressed.*

Score Point 2

Responses that are only marginally successful in clarifying, explaining, or providing information about the specified topic.

- *The "2" category is composed of the following kinds of responses:*

  ✓ *Papers that present a long list of unelaborated ideas, some of which are specific.*

  ✓ *Papers that present many ideas, most of which are extended.*

  ✓ *Papers that present just a few ideas, at least one of which is somewhat elaborated.*

Holistic Scale: Four Points *(continued)*

✓ *Papers that only summarize ideas; these papers exhibit no real elaboration.*

- *The following descriptions characterize a "2" response:*

  ✓ *A great volume of writing that is not informative in purpose.*

  ✓ *An organizational plan that does not demonstrate a logical progression of thought; such a response may also exhibit obvious repetition of ideas.* Usually, these inconsistencies do not impede the reader's understanding.

  ✓ *Marginal control of written language.* Such responses exhibit awkward or simplistic sentence structures and limited word choices. Some errors in spelling, capitalization, punctuation, and/or usage may appear, although these errors do not impede the reader's understanding.

  ✓ *A limited understanding of the topic or informative task specified in the prompt.*

Score Point 1

Responses that are unsuccessful efforts to clarify, explain, or present information about the specified topic.

- *The following types of responses fall into the "1" category:*

  ✓ *Papers in which the writer has employed the wrong mode or misunderstood his or her purpose in writing.* Some of these responses may be persuasive rather than informative. In other responses, the writer does not make any effort to address the specified audience.

  ✓ *Papers in which the writer attempts to provide expository writing, but does so unsuccessfully.* These responses may appear as any of the following forms:

    – *A brief phrase that is related to the prompt.*

    – *An overly general response.* Such responses may present one or more ideas, sometimes slightly extended or elaborated, yet they do not address the prompt in any specific or meaningful way. These responses may often appear in the form of a summary or list.

    – *A paper that initially focuses on the task but then drifts from the specified topic or from the specified purpose or mode.*

  ✓ *Papers that lack clarity.* Incomplete or illogical thoughts impede the reader's understanding. In addition, ideas are not connected in explicit or even implicit ways; the reader is confused or completely stymied in comprehending the response.

  ✓ *Papers in which the writer demonstrates no control of written language.* The reader's comprehension of the paper is seriously impeded by persistent errors in spelling, capitalization, punctuation, and usage.

  ✓ *Papers that demonstrate no organization or logic.* Such responses may present information in a random or repetitive fashion.

  ✓ *Papers that show little or no understanding of the topic or informative task specified in the prompt.*

Holistic Scale: Four Points

Score Point 4

Responses that are organized, elaborated, and highly readable attempts to present and explain an evaluation of a book. Although a "4" paper may exhibit a few inconsistencies, such inconsistencies are eclipsed by the overall quality, coherence, and thoughtfulness of the response.

- *These responses offer a clear recommendation and offer ample and convincing support for that recommendation; all reasons and evidence are relevant and well elaborated. Such responses are also characterized by most of the following:*
  - ✓ *A unified organizational plan.* These responses have a clear organization and seem complete.
  - ✓ *A marked command of written language.* These responses are fluent and clear; although some writers may not use all of the appropriate conventions of language, these responses are nevertheless quite skillfully written.
  - ✓ *Particularly thoughtful or original reasons.* Such criteria may be uncommon or exceptionally insightful rather than general or obvious. The reasons may also show a command of literary concepts and elements.
  - ✓ *Vivid, relevant details.* All descriptions and assessments are communicated through precise, effective word choices.
  - ✓ *An unusual writing strategy—one that departs from the usual or shows a spark of creative thinking.*
  - ✓ *Use of correct letter format and a clear conception of a specific audience.*
  - ✓ *Attention to all parts of the prompt.*

Score Point 3

Responses that are good efforts in addressing the hybrid task of explaining an opinion about a book and making a recommendation. For the most part, a reader finds the paper clear, coherent, and reasonably elaborated.

- *The following types of responses fall into the "3" category:*
  - ✓ *Papers that offer many reasons in support of the writer's evaluation; one may be moderately elaborated, several may be somewhat elaborated, or most may be extended.*
  - ✓ *Papers that offer at least two moderately elaborated supporting reasons.*
  - ✓ *Responses that present only one fully elaborated reason.*

- *These papers have the following characteristics:*
  - ✓ *A reasonably consistent organizational plan.* Occasional inconsistencies may be evident. Responses may also include extraneous or loosely related material.
  - ✓ *Control of written language.* Some errors in spelling, capitalization, punctuation, and/or usage may appear, but they do not unduly distract the reader.
  - ✓ *An attempt at letter format, though it may not be entirely correct, and a conception of audience, though it may be inconsistent at times.*
  - ✓ *A moderate understanding of literary elements and an ability to discuss them with reasonable skill.*

Score Point 2

Responses that are only marginally successful attempts to recommend a course of action and explain the reasons for the recommendation.

- *The following types of responses fall into the "2" category:*
  - ✓ *Papers that present a long list of unelaborated reasons, some of which are specific.*
  - ✓ *Papers that present a number of reasons, most of which are extended.*

Holistic Scale: Four Points (continued)

✓ *Papers that present a few reasons, one of which is somewhat elaborated.*

✓ *Papers that present one moderately elaborated reason.*

- *The following descriptions characterize a "2" response:*

  ✓ *Writing that is not persuasive or explanatory in purpose.*

  ✓ *An organizational plan that does not demonstrate a logical progression of thought; such a response may also exhibit obvious repetition of ideas.*

  ✓ *Marginal control of written language.* Such responses exhibit awkward or simplistic sentence structures and limited word choices. Some errors in spelling, capitalization, punctuation, and/or usage may appear, although these errors do not impede the reader's understanding.

  ✓ *No attempt at letter format beyond greeting or closing and no clear concept of audience.*

  ✓ *A limited understanding of literary elements.*

  ✓ *A limited understanding of the prompt.*

Score Point 1

Responses that are unsuccessful attempts to form or communicate an evaluation.

- *The following types of responses fall into the "1" category:*

  ✓ *Papers in which the writer has employed the wrong mode or misunderstood his or her purpose in writing.* Some of these responses may narrative rather than persuasive or explanatory. In other responses, the writer gives information that does not support his or her evaluation.

  ✓ *Papers in which the writer attempts to provide persuasive writing, but does so unsuccessfully.* These responses may appear as any of the following forms:

    —*A brief phrase that is related to the prompt.*

    —*An overly general response.* Such responses may present an evaluation statement and one or more slightly extended reasons, yet the paper does not provide a logical or meaningful case in support of the evaluation. Such responses may appear as summaries or lists.

    —*Responses that drift from the specified topic or from the task of recommending a course of action.*

  ✓ *Papers that lack clarity.* Incomplete or illogical thoughts impede the reader's understanding.

  ✓ *Papers in which the writer demonstrates no control of written language.* The reader's comprehension of the paper is seriously impeded by persistent errors in spelling, capitalization, punctuation, and usage.

  ✓ *Papers that demonstrate no organization or logic.* Information may appear in a random or repetitive way.

  ✓ *Papers that make no attempt at letter format beyond greeting or closing and have no clear conception of audience.*

  ✓ *Papers that show little or no understanding of the task called for in the prompt, including the ability to analyze literary elements.*

Analytical Scale: Six Traits

IDEAS AND CONTENT

Score 5

The paper is clear, focused, and engaging. Its thoughtful, concrete details capture the reader's attention and flesh out the central theme, main idea, or storyline.

- *A score "5" paper has the following characteristics.*

  ✓ The topic is clearly focused and manageable for a paper of its kind; it is not overly broad or scattered.
  ✓ Ideas are original and creative.
  ✓ The writer appears to be working from personal knowledge or experience.
  ✓ Key details are insightful and well-considered; they are not obvious, predictable, or humdrum.
  ✓ The development of the topic is thorough and purposeful; the writer anticipates and answers the reader's questions.
  ✓ Supporting details are never superfluous or merely ornamental; every detail contributes to the whole.

Score 3

The writer develops the topic in a general or basic way; although clear, the paper remains routine or broad.

- *A score "3" paper has the following characteristics.*

  ✓ Although the topic may be fuzzy, it is still possible to understand the writer's purpose and to predict how the paper will be developed.
  ✓ Support is present, but somewhat vague and unhelpful in illustrating the key issues or main idea; the writer makes references to his or her own experience or knowledge, but has difficulty moving from general observations to specifics.
  ✓ Ideas are understandable, yet not detailed, elaborated upon, or personalized; the writer's ideas do not reveal any deep comprehension of the topic or of the writing task.
  ✓ The writer does not stray from the topic, but ideas remain general or slightly implicit; more information is necessary to sketch in the gaps.

Score 1

The paper does not exhibit any clear purpose or main idea. The reader must use the scattered details to infer a coherent and meaningful message.

- *A score "1" paper has the following characteristics.*

  ✓ The writer seems not to have truly settled on a topic; the essay reads like a series of brainstorming notes or disconnected, random thoughts.
  ✓ The thesis is a vague statement of the topic rather than a main idea about the topic; in addition, there is little or no support or detail.
  ✓ Information is very limited or vague; readers must make inferences to fill in gaps of logic or to identify any progression of ideas.
  ✓ Text may be rambling and repetitious; alternatively, the length may not be adequate for a thoughtful development of ideas.
  ✓ There is no subordination of ideas; every idea seems equally weighted or ideas are not tied to an overarching idea.

ORGANIZATION

Score 5

Organization enables the clear communication of the central idea or storyline. The order of information draws the reader effortlessly through the text.

- *A score "5" paper has the following characteristics.*

  ✓ The sequencing is logical and effective; ideas and details "fit " where the writer has placed them.
  ✓ The essay contains an interesting or inviting introduction and a satisfying conclusion.
  ✓ The pacing is carefully controlled; the writer slows down to provide explanation or elaboration when appropriate and increases the pace when necessary.
  ✓ Transitions carefully connect ideas and cue the reader to specific relationships between ideas.
  ✓ The choice of organizational structure is appropriate to the writer's purpose and audience.
  ✓ If present, the title sums up the central idea of the paper in a fresh or thoughtful way.

Score 3

Organization is reasonably strong; it enables the reader to continually move forward without undue confusion.

- *A score "3" paper has the following characteristics.*

  ✓ The essay has an introduction and conclusion. However, the introduction may not be inviting or engaging; the conclusion may not knit all the paper's ideas together with a summary or restatement.
  ✓ Sequencing is logical, but predictable. Sometimes, the sequence may be so formulaic that it distracts from the content.
  ✓ At times, the sequence may not consistently support the essay's ideas; the reader may wish to mentally reorder sections or to supply transitions as he or she reads.
  ✓ Pacing is reasonably well done, although sometimes the writer moves ahead too quickly or spends too much time on unimportant details.
  ✓ At times, transitions may be fuzzy, showing unclear connections between ideas.
  ✓ If present, the title may be dull or a simple restatement of the topic or prompt.

Score 1

Writing does not exhibit a sense of purpose or writing strategy. Ideas, details, or events appear to be cobbled together without any internal structure.

- *A score "1" paper has the following characteristics.*

  ✓ Sequencing needs work; one idea or event does not logically follow another. Organizational problems make it difficult for the reader to understand the main idea.
  ✓ There is no real introduction to guide the reader into the paper; neither is there any real conclusion or attempt to tie things up at the end.
  ✓ Pacing is halting or inconsistent; the writer may slow the pace or speed up at inappropriate times.
  ✓ Ideas are connected with confusing transitions; alternatively, connections are altogether absent.
  ✓ If present, the title does not accurately reflect the content of the essay.

Analytical Scale: Six Traits *(continued)*

VOICE

Score 5

The writing is expressive and engaging. In addition, the writer seems to have a clear awareness of audience and purpose.

- *A score "5" paper has the following characteristics.*

  - ✓ The tone of the writing is appropriate for the purpose and audience of the paper.
  - ✓ The reader is aware of a real person behind the text; if appropriate, the writer takes risks in revealing a personal dimension throughout the piece.
  - ✓ If expository or persuasive, the writer shows a strong connection to the topic and explains why the reader should care about the issue.
  - ✓ If narrative writing, the point of view is sincere, interesting, and compelling.

Score 3

The writer is reasonably genuine, but does not reveal any excitement or connection with the issue. The resulting paper is pleasant, but not truly engaging.

- *A score "3" paper has the following characteristics.*

  - ✓ The writer offers obvious generalities instead of personal insights.
  - ✓ The writer uses neutral language and a slightly flattened tone.
  - ✓ The writer communicates in an earnest and pleasing manner, yet takes no risks. In only rare instances is the reader captivated or moved.
  - ✓ Expository or persuasive writing does not reveal a consistent engagement with the topic; there is no attempt to build credibility with the audience.
  - ✓ Narrative writing doesn't reveal a fresh or individual perspective.

Score 1

Writing is mechanical or wooden. The writer appears indifferent to the topic and/or the audience.

- *A score "1" paper has the following characteristics.*

  - ✓ The writer shows no concern with the audience; the voice may be jarringly inappropriate for the intended reader.
  - ✓ The development of the topic is so limited that no identifiable point of view is present; or the writing is so short that it offers little but a general introduction of the topic.
  - ✓ The writer seems to speak in a monotone, using a voice that suppresses all excitement about the message.
  - ✓ Although the writing may communicate on a functional level, the writing is ordinary and takes no risks; depending on the topic, it may be overly technical or jargonistic.

WORD CHOICE

Score 5

Words are precise, engaging, and unaffected. They convey the writer's message in an interesting and effective way.

■ *A score "5" paper has the following characteristics.*

✓ All words are specific and appropriate. In all instances, the writer has taken care to choose the right words or phrases.

✓ The paper's language is natural, not overwrought; it never shows a lack of control. Clichés and jargon are rarely used.

✓ The paper contains energetic verbs; precise nouns and modifiers provide clarity.

✓ The writer uses vivid words and phrases, including sensory details; such language creates distinct images in the reader's mind.

Score 3

Despite its lack of flair, the paper's language gets the message across. It is functional and clear.

■ *A score "3" paper has the following characteristics.*

✓ Words are correct and generally adequate, but lack originality or precision.

✓ Familiar words and phrases do not pique the reader's interest or imagination. Lively verbs and phrases perk things up occasionally, but the paper does not consistently sparkle.

✓ There are attempts at engaging or academic language but they sometimes seem overly showy or pretentious.

✓ The writing contains passive verbs, basic nouns and adjectives, and the lack of precise adverbs.

Score 1

The writer's limited vocabulary impedes communication; he or she seems to struggle for words to convey a clear message.

■ *A score "1" paper has the following characteristics.*

✓ Vague language communicates an imprecise or incomplete message. The reader is left confused or unsure of the writer's purpose.

✓ Words are used incorrectly. In addition, frequent misuse of parts of speech impair understanding.

✓ Excessive redundancy in the paper is distracting.

✓ The writing overuses jargon or clichés.

Analytical Scale: Six Traits *(continued)*

SENTENCE FLUENCY

Score 5

Sentences are thoughtfully constructed and sentence structure is varied throughout the paper. When read aloud, the writing is fluent and rhythmic.

■ *A score "5" paper has the following characteristics.*

✓ The sentences are constructed so that meaning is clear to the reader.

✓ Sentences vary in length and in structure.

✓ Varied sentence beginnings add interest and clarity.

✓ The writing has a steady beat; the reader is able to read the text effortlessly, without confusion or stumbling.

✓ Dialogue, if used, is natural. Any fragments are used purposefully and contribute to the paper's style.

✓ Thoughtful connectives and transitions between sentences reveal how the paper's ideas work together.

Score 3

The text maintains a steady rhythm, but the reader may find it more flat or mechanical than fluent or musical.

■ *A score "3" paper has the following characteristics.*

✓ Sentences are usually grammatical and unified, but they are routine rather than artful. The writer has not paid a great deal of attention to how the sentences sound.

✓ There is some variation in sentence length and structure as well as in sentence beginnings. Not all sentences are constructed exactly the same way.

✓ The reader may have to search for transitional words and phrases that show how sentences relate to one another. Sometimes, such context clues are entirely absent when they should be present.

✓ Although sections of the paper invite expressive oral reading, the reader may also encounter many wooden or awkward sections.

Score 1

The reader will encounter challenges in reading the choppy or confusing text; meaning may be significantly obscured by the errors in sentence construction.

■ *A score "1" paper has the following characteristics.*

✓ The sentences do not "hang together." They are run-on, incomplete, monotonous, or awkward.

✓ Phrasing often sounds too sing-song, not natural. The paper does not invite expressive oral reading.

✓ Nearly all the sentences begin the same way and they may all follow the same pattern (e.g., subject-verb-object). The result may be a monotonous repetition of sounds.

✓ Endless connectives or a complete lack of connectives create a confused muddle of language.

Analytical Scale: Six Traits *(continued)*

CONVENTIONS

Score 5

Standard writing conventions (e.g., spelling, punctuation, capitalization, grammar, usage, and paragraphing) are used correctly and in a way that aids the reader's understanding. Any errors tend to be minor; the piece is nearly ready for publication.

- A score "5" paper has the following characteristics.

  ✓ Paragraphing is regular and enhances the organization of the paper.

  ✓ Grammar and usage are correct and add clarity to the text as a whole. Sometimes, the writer may manipulate conventions in a controlled way—especially grammar and spelling—for stylistic effect.

  ✓ Punctuation is accurate; it enables the reader to move through the text with understanding and ease.

  ✓ The writer's understanding of capitalization skills is evident throughout the paper.

  ✓ Most words, even difficult ones, are spelled correctly.

Score 3

The writer exhibits an awareness of a limited set of standard writing conventions and uses them to enhance the paper's readability. Although the writer shows control, at times errors distract the reader or impede communication. Moderate editing is required for publication.

- A score "3" paper has the following characteristics.

  ✓ Paragraphs are used, but may begin in the wrong places or run together sections that should be separate paragraphs.

  ✓ Conventions may not be correct all of the time. However, problems with grammar and usage are usually not serious enough to distort meaning.

  ✓ Terminal (end-of-sentence) punctuation is usually correct; internal punctuation (e.g. commas, apostrophes, semicolons, parentheses) may be missing or wrong.

  ✓ On common words, spelling is usually correct or phonetic.

  ✓ Most words are capitalized correctly, but the writer's command of more sophisticated capitalization skills is inconsistent.

Score 1

There are errors in spelling, punctuation, usage and grammar, capitalization, and/or paragraphing that seriously impede the reader's comprehension. Extensive editing is required for publication.

- A score "1" paper has the following characteristics.

  ✓ Paragraphing is missing, uneven, or too frequent. Most of the paragraphs do not reinforce or support the organizational structure of the paper.

  ✓ Errors in grammar/usage are very common and distracting; such errors also affect the paper's meaning.

  ✓ Punctuation, including terminal punctuation, is often missing or incorrect.

  ✓ Even on common words, spelling errors are frequent.

  ✓ Capitalization is haphazard or reveals the writer's understanding of only the simplest rules.

  ✓ The paper must be read once just to decode the language and then again to capture the paper's meaning.

Notes on Writing Assessment Scales

Use this page to extend and adjust the criteria for writing provided in the scales on pages 145–158. Or just jot some notes about criteria you want to pay special attention to as you read the essays ahead.

_____

_____

_____

_____

_____

_____

_____

_____

_____

_____

_____

_____

_____

_____

_____

_____

_____

_____

_____

_____

_____

_____

_____

_____

_____

_____

_____

_____

_____

_____

_____

_____

_____

_____

_____

Sample A: Expository Writing

PROMPT

Think about the seasons of the year. Do you prefer summer, spring, autumn, or winter? Write a well-organized paper telling which season you prefer and why.

No TEACHERS + No HOMEWORK + NOTHING to worry about = My favorite season SUMMER. Once you get into summer you take these things for granted, all because you have much better things to think about and do. The main reasons I like summer are Nature camp, soccer camp, and vacations.

In the summer I come home very tired because I spend most days at The Nature Center, a very involved and active camp. At the camp, other kids and I do just about everything kids could possibly want to do outdoors. For example, one activity we do is explore caves. The counselors teach us all about rock formations and animals that live in the caves. We also enjoy rock climbing. This activity can be very scary, but it strengthens your muscles and teaches you to have confidence in yourself. Another activity we do is snorkel in Lake Travis. The water is very clear so you can see many fish, mainly perch. My time at The Nature Center is very tiring, but it is also exciting.

Overnight soccer camp is also a memorable part of summer. Soccer camp teaches me to be a better soccer player because I practice all the time. From 8:00 AM to 5:00 PM it seems like all I do is RUN, RUN, RUN, and RUN some more, but I am also learning useful soccer skills. For example, I learned how to fool an opponent by faking a pass in one direction and then dribbling in another direction. I also learned how to tackle or kick the ball away from an opponent and still keep the ball. In spite of all the hard work, soccer camp has its "crazy" times. After a long day of practicing everyone jumps in the coldest pool in Austin, known as Barton Springs. Believe me when I say it is one of the most refreshing feelings. Soccer camp is a great part of summer.

Sample A: Expository Writing *(continued)*

You're probably wondering if I go on any trips. My family has started a tradition where we go to a family reunion at my uncle's bay house on the Gulf of Mexico. We go every summer, and every time I always have the time of my life. My cousins and I spend the days swimming in the ocean, crabbing, and fishing. Last summer I caught an eight pound Speckled Trout. My uncle had to help me pull it in the boat, but it was worth the fight because supper that night was awesome. My family also goes on trips with just the three of us. If you're thinking BORING, guess again. Every vacation we go on together has been an incredible amount of fun because I don't have to worry about acting perfect all the time.

Summer is definitely my favorite season. I enjoy Nature camp, soccer camp, and vacations. If you really want to know, I like summer so much I'm counting the days until the next summer begins.

Sample A Evaluation: Expository Writing

Six Point Holistic Scale

Rating: 6 points

Comments: The paper clearly focuses on the topic and the expository purpose. Organization is consistent and logical, with each reason presented in a separate paragraph. The writer provides specific and relevant details to support the main idea of each body paragraph; however, the fourth paragraph includes a statement about "acting perfect" that might have been more fully elaborated. The writer's voice is engaging, and his references to "you" are a clue to his awareness of audience. The writer also uses a variety of sentences and shows a control of written language, making few errors in mechanics, usage, and punctuation.

Four Point Holistic Scale

Rating: 4 points

Comments: The paper presents ideas in an engaging and focused way throughout. The organizational strategy is clear and complete with the main idea stated in the introduction, supported in the body paragraphs, and restated in the conclusion. The writer provides well-elaborated reasons that move from the general to specific, vivid details. This is especially evident in the second and third paragraphs. The fourth paragraph, though, ends with a reason that is not as fully developed. Sentences are varied, and word choice is effective. The writer shows control of written language as characterized by few punctuation and usage mistakes.

Six Trait Analytic Scale

Ratings

Ideas and Content: 4	**Word Choice: 4**
Organization: 5	**Sentence Fluency: 5**
Voice: 5	**Conventions: 5**

Comments: The paper is clearly focused on explaining why summer is the writer's favorite season. The writer provides specific details and anecdotes to develop the reasons, although development is occasionally lacking. For example, the reader has to guess as to what the writer means by not "acting perfect all the time." Organization is logical and coherent and the topic sentences in the introduction and the body paragraphs prepare the reader for what is to come. The writer's voice is engaging and appropriate for an informative purpose. Word choice is good, using energetic verbs and precise words and phrases. Sentence structure is varied and creates an easy-to-read rhythm. The writer demonstrates a good understanding of the conventions of written language and even experiments with conventions for effect, as shown in the first sentence.

Sample B: Expository Writing

PROMPT

Think about the seasons of the year. Do you prefer summer, spring, autumn, or winter? Write a well-organized paper telling which season you prefer and why.

Out of all the seasons I would have to say that my favorite one is summer. Three things that make summer more enjoyable are 1. No TEACHERS, 2. No HOME-WORK, and finally 3. Nothing to worry about. Once you get into summer you just take those things for granted, all because you have much better things to think about. The main reasons I like summer are soccer, camps, and more soccer.

Usually I would come home dog tired. The reason for this is that while I'm going to The Nature Center (a very involved and active camp) we would do just about every-thing a kid could possibly want to do outdoors. You do things like caving.

Overnight soccer camps are some of the most vivid memories of my many sum-mers. During the time period from 8:00 AM to 5:00 PM we did pretty much noth-ing but RUN, RUN, RUN, and RUN some more. I had never in my entire life run so much at one time. In spite of all the hard work it had its perks. For example after we had been running for what seemed like forever we had the pleasure of jumping in the coldest pool in Austin, known as Barton Springs.

The one thing so far that you're probably wondering is "don't you go on any trips?" There is certainly always a great urge to travel and especially to another country. We have started going to the family reunion. We have always gone to my uncle's bay house on the Gulf of Mexico for part of the summer. Every time we go I always have the time of my life. Last but not least on my list is family vacations of just the three of us, one "big" happy family. If you're thinking BORING, guess again. Every vacation that we went on together so far has been an incredible amount of fun because I don't have to worry about acting totally perfectly good all the time.

Soccer, action, and outdoors makes summer fun for me.

Sample B Evaluation: Expository Writing

Six Point Holistic Scale

Rating: 4 points

Comments: The writer generally focuses on the topic, but provides support that is only moderately elaborated. An overall organizational strategy is apparent by the use of separate paragraphs for an introduction, each reason, and a conclusion. However, the development of ideas within the paragraphs is sometimes flawed by a lack of unity. The writer generally follows the conventions of mechanics, usage, and grammar, and is able to use nonstandard capitalization and other stylistic experiments to communicate a lively voice and tone.

Four Point Holistic Scale

Rating: 3 points

Comments: The writer makes a good attempt to address the prompt. Clear reasons support the writer's preference; however, they are only extended or somewhat elaborated. The writer follows an organizational pattern, placing each reason in a separate paragraph. Within the paragraphs, though, ideas are sometimes loosely related. Sentence structure is somewhat varied and the writer has a general control of the written language, as characterized by few punctuation and usage errors.

Six Trait Analytic Scale

Ratings

Ideas and Content: 3	**Word Choice: 3**
Organization: 3	**Sentence Fluency: 3**
Voice: 4	**Conventions: 4**

Comments: The writer's preference for summer is easily recognized. Reasons are provided, but support for each reason is underdeveloped. Organization is predictable, and the transition between ideas is sometimes fuzzy. The writer's word choices are adequate, using familiar words and phrases. The voice, though, is engaging and clearly expresses the writer's excitement and involvement with the topic. The writer uses varied sentence structure and demonstrates an understanding of standard written conventions.

Sample C: Expository Writing

> **PROMPT**
>
> Think about the seasons of the year. Do you prefer summer, spring, autumn, or winter? Write a well-organized paper telling which season you prefer and why.

The things that make summer more enjoyable is nothing to worry about.

Usually I would come home tired. The reason for this is that while I'm going to The Nature Center we would do just about everything a kid or even an adult could possibly want to do outdoors. But why would I go to play soccer for only two hours when I can play soccer all day at soccer camp.

I have always loved soccer ever since kindergarten; even though I didn't play on a team that year. A part of my summer is spent on soccer tournaments. Even though they don't happen that often.

Conditioning was not one of my favorite parts of summer. During the time period from 8:00 AM to 5:00 PM we did pretty much nothing but run. I had never in my entire life run so much at one time. I was really close to quitting. In spite of all the hard work it has its perks.

The one thing so far that you're probably wondering is "don't you go on any trips?" You would have to be completely out of your mind if you thought that we never go on vacations. Last but not least on my list is family vacations of just the three of us, one "big" happy family. Every vacation that we went on together so far has been an incredible amount of fun because I don't have to worry about acting totally perfectly good all the time.

Soccer makes summer fun for me.

Sample C Evaluation: Expository Writing

Six Point Holistic Scale

Rating: 2 points

Comments: The writer generally focuses on the topic, but does include extraneous information, as shown in the third paragraph. An organizational pattern is attempted but lacks unity overall. Paragraphing is not always used correctly, either. For example, the second paragraph contains two topics, the Nature Center and soccer. In addition, reasons given in the body paragraphs provide weak support for the main idea stated in the introduction. Sentences are somewhat varied; however, diction is basic and the writer does not demonstrate a clear understanding of punctuation. Other usage problems are also apparent, such as inconsistencies with subject-verb agreement and verb tense.

Four Point Holistic Scale

Rating: 2 points

Comments: The writer makes a minimal attempt to address the prompt. Reasons are given for the writer's preference, but they are only extended or summarized. For example, the writer discusses vacations in the fourth paragraph but does not provide any specific details to elaborate on the idea. Furthermore, even though the reader can understand the writer's preference for summer, the organizational strategy is flawed by a lack of unity. Irrelevant details such as those in the third paragraph interrupt the reasons. The paper also contains some distracting errors in punctuation and usage.

Six Trait Analytic Scale

Ratings

Ideas and Content: 2	**Word Choice: 2**
Organization: 2	**Sentence Fluency: 2**
Voice: 3	**Conventions: 3**

Comments: The writer has difficulty developing the topic fully, providing only a minimal amount of support. In addition, information does not always seem connected. For example, the reader must assume that "conditioning" is part of the soccer camp mentioned in the second paragraph. Organization is attempted, but details still seem loosely strung together. The writer's voice is pleasant but not very unique or compelling. Word choice is adequate, and sentences are somewhat varied. The writer has reasonable control over the conventions of writing, but the paper does contain errors in punctuation, grammar, and paragraphing.

Notes on Expository Writing

Use this page to jot notes about the expository essays or evaluations you have just read. How would you evaluate the essays?

_____

_____

_____

_____

_____

_____

_____

_____

_____

_____

_____

_____

_____

_____

_____

_____

_____

_____

_____

_____

_____

_____

_____

_____

Sample A: Friendly Letter of Recommendation

PROMPT

Have you ever read a book that you wanted to share with others?
Choose a fiction, nonfiction, or poetry book that you enjoyed reading and
write a friendly letter recommending it. Address your recommendation to
a reader of your choice.

Dear Stephanie,

How are you doing in the 6th grade? My year is going perfectly. I like all of my teachers, especially my reading teacher. We have to read one hour and thirty minutes each week. I just finished reading a great book called the <u>Search for Senna.</u>

I recommend you read this book and the rest of the <u>Everworld</u> series because it starts fast, and uses words that give a good mental picture. The series is about a group of teenagers who discover a world where all of the myths from Vikings to Aztecs and everything in between are real. The author, K.A. Applegate, leaves you in suspense and waiting to read the sequel.

Some books can tell you their whole life story before any type of action happens. In the <u>Search for Senna</u> it is summed up in a few sentences and then the first real event happens. Also it is always one event after another. Never are there any recaps told. Have you ever been riding in a car to get something special and you just can't get there fast enough? Well that is what it is like trying to get to the next page. After reading page three, I locked myself in my room until I was done. Now I have started pacing myself though, which is a good thing because K.A. Applegate is still working on book five, and I have been done with book four for three months.

K.A. Applegate must have written the dictionary. The words she uses and the way she uses them could make you think so. Mythical words like Loki, Norseman, Fenrir,

Sample A: Friendly Letter of Recommendation *(cont.)*

Ka Anor, and wonderous words like carburtor, treacherous, and tantalizing. All of these words and many more weave a web containing a picture of unbelievable visual reality. In such a visual reality you can lose your breath just trying to control the beautiful picture. My words flitter and flutter through my mouth just writing of it. The words are truley that creative!

All of the _Everworld_ books get you to the true height of one adventure and leave you hanging and digging through a drawer for money for the sequel, _Land of Loss_. She leaves you in so much suspense you are hooked to a ball and chain with the key in a bookstore at the cost of four dollars and ninety-nine cents.

Those are but a few of the reasons that I recommend you read the _Search for Senna_ and all of the _Everworld_ books. The great suspense thrills, mental pictures and the speedy beginning are realy what made that book good. So stick your nose in a book, I suggest _Everworld_.

Sample A Evaluation: Friendly Letter of Recommendation

Six Point Holistic Scale

Rating: 6 points

Comments: The letter is clear, engaging, and well organized. The writer's reasons clearly support the recommendation and are based on thoughtful criteria, including suspense and vivid descriptions. Each reason is fully elaborated using analogies and examples from the book. The writer also demonstrates a strong involvement with the topic and the audience, expressing ideas in a fresh, appealing voice. Most sentences are complete except when fragments are used purposefully, and sentence structures and lengths vary. Few errors are made in mechanics, usage, and grammar, and these errors do not interfere with communication of the writer's message.

Four Point Holistic Scale

Rating: 4 points

Comments: The writer's reasons are specific, well elaborated, and clearly support the recommendation. The letter is organized in a logical way and has a sense of completeness. The writer has also shown an awareness of common criteria for evaluating books, including the pace of the plot. In addition, she has provided a brief, helpful summary of the *Everworld* series. The writer's word choice is highly effective, with strong analogies and vivid expressions. The writer also demonstrates control over written language; the few errors in spelling, grammar, and usage are eclipsed by the overall fluency of the response.

Six Trait Analytic Scale

Ratings

Ideas and Content: 5	**Word Choice: 4**
Organization: 4	**Sentence Fluency: 5**
Voice: 5	**Conventions: 5**

Comments: The writer develops the topic in a fresh and purposeful way. Organization is clear and logical, though transitions between major ideas are missing. The writer's voice is lively and shows a strong awareness of audience and purpose. Word choice is vivid and striking, although some passages are slightly overdone. Sentences vary in structure and length and most are complete except when fragments are used purposefully. Paragraphing is sound. Grammar, usage, punctuation, and spelling are generally correct.

Sample B: Friendly Letter of Recommendation

PROMPT

Have you ever read a book that you wanted to share with others? Choose a fiction, nonfiction, or poetry book that you enjoyed reading and write a friendly letter recommending it. Address your recommendation to a reader of your choice.

Dear Stephanie,

    I just finished reading a great book called the <u>Search for Senna</u>. I recommend you read this book and the rest of the <u>Everworld</u> series because it starts fast, and gives a good mental picture. K.A. Applegate leaves you in suspense and waiting to read the sequel without much profanity.

    Some books can tell you their whole life story before any type of action happens. In the <u>Search for Senna</u> it is summed up in a few sentences and the first real event happens. Also it is always one event after another. Never are there any recaps told. After reading page three, I locked myself in my room until I was done. Now I have started pacing myself though. Which is a good thing because K.A. Applegate is still working on book five, and I have been done with book four for three months.

    K.A. Applegate uses words like Loki, Norseman, Fenrir, Ka Anor, carburtor, treacherous, and tantalizing. All of these words and many more create a vivid mental picture. The words are truley that creative!

    All of the Everword get you to the true height of one adventure and leave you hanging and digging through a drawer for money for the sequal, <u>Land of Loss</u>. It is like being suspended from Golden Gate bridge from a bungie cord made of lead. She leaves you in so much suspense your hooked to a ball and chain with the key in a bookstore at the cost of four dollars and ninety-nine. You know how they say that curiosity killed the cat? Well, if money were curiosity bye-bye kitty cat.

Sample B: Friendly Letter of Recommendation *(cont.)*

In such a wonderful book described as above by an eleven year old you probably think that they go through saying "Well, beep!", "Beep; Beep; Beeeep!", but they don't. In fact there are not hardly any profanity. What ever little you find would not fit on a quarter.

Those are but a few of the reasons that I recommend you read the <u>Search for Senna</u> and all of the Everworld books. The small profanity, great suspense thrills, mental pictures and the speedy beginning are realy what made that book a good book to read not this paper. So stick your nose in a book, I suggest <u>Everworld</u>.

Sample B Evaluation: Friendly Letter of Recommendation

Six Point Holistic Scale

Rating: 4 points

Comments: The recommendation is clear and supported by several reasons that are extended or somewhat elaborated. The writer's criteria for evaluation are thoughtful and show an awareness of the qualities of a book her audience might care about. The organization is clear, though the paper lacks explicit transitions between ideas. Most sentences are complete, and diction is adequate if sometimes too flowery. The letter generally follows conventions of mechanics, usage, and grammar, and any errors do not interfere with the message.

Four Point Holistic Scale

Rating: 3 points

Comments: The recommendation is supported by several reasons that are extended or somewhat elaborated. Organization is logical, although ideas are not always clearly connected. The letter generally adheres to letter format and exhibits general control of written language, with only minor errors in spelling, capitalization, punctuation, and usage. However, the writer's frequent use of figurative language is somewhat overdone and confusing.

Six Trait Analytic Scale

Ratings

Ideas and Content: 4	**Word Choice: 4**
Organization: 3	**Sentence Fluency: 3**
Voice: 4	**Conventions: 3**

Comments: The writer includes some fresh ideas, though support in the letter is not fully developed. Organization is logical, but transitions between ideas are missing, making the paper somewhat confusing to read. The writer's voice reveals the person behind the words but sometimes becomes obscured in the confusing series of metaphors. Word choice is accurate and at times lively. Most sentences are complete, although some awkward sentences are present. Errors in grammar, usage, punctuation, and spelling do not seriously interfere with the letter's message.

STUDENT MODEL

Sample C: Friendly Letter of Recommendation

Copyright © by Holt, Rinehart and Winston. All rights reserved.

PROMPT

Have you ever read a book that you wanted to share with others? Choose a fiction, nonfiction, or poetry book that you enjoyed reading and write a friendly letter recommending it. Address your recommendation to a reader of your choice.

I just finished reading a great book called the Search for Senna. It starts fast, and K.A. Applegate leaves you in suspense and waiting to read the sequel. It is in a series called Everworld.

Some books can tell you their whole life story before any type of action happens. In the Search for Senna it is summed up in a few sentences and the first real event happens. Also it is always one event after another.

K.A. Applegate uses alot of creative words like Loki, Norseman, and tantalizing. All of these words and many more are truley creative. Some authors never use creative words like these.

All of the Everword leave you hanging and digging through a drawer for money for the sequel. She leaves you in suspense so you have to go in a bookstore and spend four dollars and ninety-nine. Some books are more expensive, though. She also wrote the Animorphs.

You probably think that in the book they go through saying "Well, beep!", "Beep; Beep; Beeeep!", but they don't. In fact there are not hardly any profanity. I have read other book that use much more profanity than this. So it was a good book.

Sample C Evaluation: Friendly Letter of Recommendation

Six Point Holistic Scale

Rating: 2 points

Comments: The response addresses the topic but contains information that is irrelevant and not persuasive in purpose. A weak recommendation is supported by reasons that are somewhat extended. The letter feels incomplete and shows little involvement with the audience. Word choice is limited or vague. The letter shows limited control of written language, with awkward and incorrect sentences and errors in grammar, usage, punctuation, and spelling. Letter format is completely absent.

Four Point Holistic Scale

Rating: 1 point

Comments: The response addresses the topic with a weak recommendation, poorly elaborated support, and little connection between ideas. Organization is somewhat random and illogical. It is occasionally difficult to determine what the letter's message is. The letter also shows the writer's limited control of written language, with awkward sentence structures, poor word choices, and errors in spelling, capitalization, punctuation, and usage. Letter format is absent, as is any clear or consistent awareness of audience.

Six Trait Analytic Scale

Ratings

Ideas and Content: 2	**Word Choice: 2**
Organization: 2	**Sentence Fluency: 1**
Voice: 1	**Conventions: 1**

Comments: Ideas are not clearly connected, and support is limited. Organization appears random; transitions and conclusion are missing. The writer's voice is not apparent in this response, and there appears to be little awareness of an audience. Word choice is limited, though usually appropriate. Sentences are often awkward and unclear, though many are grammatical. Many errors in usage, punctuation, and spelling interfere with the writer's message.

Notes on Recommendation Letters

Use this page to jot notes about the friendly letters of recommendation that you have just read. How would you evaluate the letters?

_____

_____

_____

_____

_____

_____

_____

_____

_____

_____

_____

_____

_____

_____

_____

_____

_____

_____

_____

_____

_____

_____

_____

_____

_____

_____

Telling a Story

DIRECTIONS: Circle 1, 2, or 3 below to indicate your evaluation of each item.

Evaluation Scale:	1 = Not at all	2 = To some extent	3 = Successfully

- The student chooses an interesting incident to retell.   1   2   3

- The student tells the story in chronological order.   1   2   3

- The student provides background information needed to understand the story.   1   2   3

- The student uses notecards for speaking rather than reading a complete essay.   1   2   3

- The student uses formal English except when sharing dialogue.   1   2   3

- The student includes regional or cultural labels or sayings in dialogue.   1   2   3

- The student speaks loudly enough to be heard and enunciates words clearly.   1   2   3

- The student adds interest by varying volume and by using different voices for different characters.   1   2   3

- The student uses facial expressions effectively.   1   2   3

- The student acts out emotions and actions.   1   2   3

- The student adjusts content and delivery to maintain audience interest.   1   2   3 for **CHAPTER TWO: FOCUS ON VIEWING AND REPRESENTING**   page 76   **RUBRIC**

Producing a Newspaper

DIRECTIONS: Circle 1, 2, or 3 below to indicate your evaluation of each item.

Evaluation Scale:	1 = Not at all	2 = To some extent	3 = Successfully

- Students divide tasks equitably.   1   2   3

- The newspaper's front page includes a flag identifying the paper's title and publication date.   1   2   3

- The newspaper includes student-written articles on school news in a separate section.   1   2   3

- The newspaper includes student-written articles on community news in a separate section.   1   2   3

- The newspaper includes student-written editorials and a student-created editorial cartoon in a separate section.   1   2   3

- Editorial pieces include an opinion statement supported by reasons, which in turn are supported by facts and examples.   1   2   3

- The newspaper layout is effective, with articles in square or rectangular blocks and headlines clearly separated from one another.   1   2   3

- The newspaper includes at least one image related to the topic of one of its articles.   1   2   3

- The articles are word-processed or neatly written in columns.   1   2   3

- Articles too long to fit their allotted space are cut from the end.   1   2   3

Producing a TV News Segment

DIRECTIONS: Circle 1, 2, or 3 below to indicate your evaluation of each item.

▶ **Evaluation Scale:**   1 = Not at all   2 = To some extent   3 = Successfully

- Students divide tasks equitably.   1   2   3

- The chosen story is newsworthy and has visual interest.   1   2   3

- The details of the event are told clearly and completely.   1   2   3

- The producer correctly signals the camera operator, anchor, and reporter, and holds up cue cards as needed.   1   2   3

- The cameraperson operates the video equipment correctly, including starting and stopping at the appropriate points and focusing on the reporter, anchor, or visuals as needed.   1   2   3

- Camera shots are steady and clear.   1   2   3

- The anchor and reporter rarely, if ever, rely on cue cards.   1   2   3

- The anchor and reporter speak slowly, clearly, and loudly and look into the camera or at the person they are interviewing as needed.   1   2   3

- The reporter and anchor dress appropriately for their roles.   1   2   3

- Transitions between shots are smooth and the newscast flows well from beginning to end.   1   2   3

Viewing and Listening to Learn

DIRECTIONS: Circle 1, 2, or 3 below to indicate your evaluation of each item.

Evaluation Scale: 1 = Not at all   2 = To some extent   3 = Successfully

- The student is able to identify flowcharts and diagrams.   1   2   3

- The student recognizes that instructions in flowcharts and diagrams are   1   2   3
  communicated with words, symbols, and pictures.

- The student correctly identifies the order of instructions in flowcharts   1   2   3
  and diagrams.

- The student correctly translates the text in the help box provided on   1   2   3
  pupil's edition page 115 into a flowchart.

- The student's flowchart demonstrates an understanding of the instruc-   1   2   3
  tional process through appropriately placed boxes and arrows.

- The student chooses and views an appropriate "how-to" video.   1   2   3

- While viewing the video, the student takes thorough notes using the   1   2   3
  techniques provided in the pupil's edition (page 116).

- The student is able to thoughtfully answer the sentence starters in the   1   2   3
  pupil's edition (page 116).

Comparing Ideas in Photographs

DIRECTIONS: Circle 1, 2, or 3 below to indicate your evaluation of each item.

Evaluation Scale:	1 = Not at all	2 = To some extent	3 = Successfully

- The student identifies the characteristics of photographs.   1   2   3

- The student identifies a variety of media that provide information.   1   2   3

- The student recognizes the effect of changing camera angles on an image.   1   2   3

- The student recognizes that cropping can change the content and meaning of a photograph.   1   2   3

- The student identifies the attitude toward an image conveyed by its caption.   1   2   3

- The student writes captions that effectively convey an attitude toward the content of a photograph.   1   2   3

- The student thoughtfully compares the messages conveyed by two versions of the same photograph.   1   2   3

Comparing Media: Film, TV, and Literature

DIRECTIONS: Circle 1, 2, or 3 below to indicate your evaluation of each item.

Evaluation Scale:	1 = Not at all	2 = To some extent	3 = Successfully

- The student can identify examples of a variety of genres.   1   2   3

- The student chooses an appropriate book and movie or television program combination.   1   2   3

- The student correctly uses terms listed in boldface in the workshop.   1   2   3

- The student identifies tools used by authors, television and film producers, and both.   1   2   3

- The student creates charts such as those on pages 183 and 184 of the pupil's edition for the book read and movie or television program watched.   1   2   3

- The student works cooperatively with a partner.   1   2   3

- The generalization is valid and supported by information in the student's and partner's charts.   1   2   3

Giving and Evaluating a Research Presentation

DIRECTIONS: Circle 1, 2, or 3 below to indicate your evaluation of each item.

Evaluation Scale:	1 = Not at all	2 = To some extent	3 = Successfully

Speaking

- The student uses notecards listing key information about the topic rather than reading from written report.   1   2   3

- The student uses standard English.   1   2   3

- The student speaks loudly, slowly, and clearly enough to be understood.   1   2   3

- The student elaborates on ideas to explain them clearly.   1   2   3

- The student appropriately uses a visual that adds to audience understanding.   1   2   3

- The student makes eye contact with audience members.   1   2   3

- The student presents ideas in a logical order.   1   2   3

- The student uses gestures or voice modulation to emphasize important ideas.   1   2   3

- If technology is used, it contributes to the overall presentation rather than detracting from the speaker's message.   1   2   3

Listening

- The student asks questions for clarification as needed.   1   2   3

- The student makes notes on the speaker's content and delivery.   1   2   3

- The student limits distractions and focuses attention on the speaker.   1   2   3

Evaluating a Persuasive Speech

DIRECTIONS: Circle 1, 2, or 3 below to indicate your evaluation of each item.

Evaluation Scale:	1 = Not at all	2 = To some extent	3 = Successfully

- The student identifies the elements of a persuasive speech.   1 2 3

- The student identifies persuasive techniques (or propaganda techniques).   1 2 3

- The student develops appropriate criteria for evaluating the content of a persuasive speech.   1 2 3

- The student develops appropriate criteria for evaluating the delivery of a persuasive speech.   1 2 3

- The student develops appropriate criteria for evaluating the believability of a persuasive speech.   1 2 3

- The student asks questions for clarification as needed.   1 2 3

- The student makes notes to evaluate a persuasive speech based on criteria for content, delivery, and believability.   1 2 3

- The student writes an evaluation of a persuasive speech based on the criteria for content, delivery, and believability.   1 2 3

- The student participates appropriately in a small-group discussion.   1 2 3

Introduction: *Choices* Activities

Evaluation Scale:	1 = Not at all	2 = To some extent	3 = Successfully

Viewing and Representing

1. Small-Screen Sightings

- The student takes notes on a variety of television portrayals of reading and writing. — 1　2　3
- The student actively participates in a discussion about how television represents readers and writers. — 1　2　3
- The student uses notes and ideas from the discussion to develop a paragraph explaining why the student agrees or disagrees with the way television shows people reading and writing. — 1　2　3
- The paragraph is relatively free of errors in spelling, usage, grammar, and mechanics. — 1　2　3

Careers

2. In Your Dreams

- The student chooses and researches an appropriate career. — 1　2　3
- The student makes notes on how people in the chosen career field use reading and writing in their work. — 1　2　3
- The student summarizes his or her findings in an oral report. — 1　2　3
- The student speaks clearly and audibly during the report. — 1　2　3

Collaborative Writing

3. Learning Through Teaching

- The student participates appropriately in a small group. — 1　2　3
- The student helps choose a process to explore and identify an audience for the group's skit. — 1　2　3
- The student completes one or more of the tasks listed. — 1　2　3
- The skit clearly explains the chosen process to its audience. — 1　2　3

Creative Writing

4. The Choice Is Yours

- The student writes about the reading process in one of the ways listed, and generally follows the conventions of grammar, usage, punctuation, and spelling. — 1　2　3
- If the student writes a journal entry, the writing expresses the student's thoughts using reflection in the first person. — 1　2　3
- If the student writes persuasively, the editorial or review clearly states an opinion and supports it with reasons and evidence. — 1　2　3
- If the student writes an expository piece, the report, presentation, or instructions are clear, detailed, and well organized. — 1　2　3

Chapter One: *Choices* Activities

▶ **Evaluation Scale:**   1 = Not at all   2 = To some extent   3 = Successfully

Careers

1. When I Grow Up
- The student reads an appropriate biography.   1   2   3
- The student writes a journal entry that clearly and thoroughly describes   1   2   3
  one thing that surprised the student about the person and his or her career.
- The journal entry is relatively free of errors in spelling, usage, grammar,   1   2   3
  and mechanics.

Speech

2. Telling Tales
- The student reads two folk tales from different cultures.   1   2   3
- The student makes notes comparing the two folk tales.   1   2   3
- The student reflects on the culture that the folk tales originated from.   1   2   3
- The student explains the comparison in a speech, speaking clearly and   1   2   3
  audibly during the presentation.

Drama

3. Another Life
- The student helps select an appropriate play to present.   1   2   3
- With classmates, the student presents a dramatic interpretation of a play   1   2   3
  based on the life of a real person.
- The student speaks clearly, audibly, and with appropriate emphasis   1   2   3
  during the presentation.
- The student remains in character throughout the presentation.   1   2   3

Writing

4. Larger Than Life
- The student writes a tall tale.   1   2   3
- The tale includes realistic elements, but also larger-than-life details.   1   2   3
- The tale demonstrates the student's imagination and creativity.   1   2   3
- The tale is relatively free of errors in spelling, grammar, usage, and   1   2   3
  mechanics.

Technology

5. You've Got Mail
- The student sends an e-mail that describes a recent event.   1   2   3
- The description includes background information.   1   2   3
- The description is clearly and logically organized.   1   2   3
- The description is relatively free of errors in spelling, usage, grammar,   1   2   3
  and mechanics.

RUBRICS

Chapter Two: *Choices* Activities

Evaluation Scale:	1 = Not at all	2 = To some extent	3 = Successfully

Careers

1. Behind the News

- The student chooses and researches an appropriate career field. 1 2 3
- The student writes a report that clearly and thoroughly explains the education and training required and the average salary for a person in the chosen career field. 1 2 3
- The report is relatively free of errors in spelling, grammar, usage, and mechanics. 1 2 3

Crossing the Curriculum: Art

2. Express Yourself

- The student chooses an appropriate event or situation as the subject of an editorial cartoon. 1 2 3
- The student creates an editorial cartoon that clearly presents the situation or event and the student's opinion of it. 1 2 3
- The cartoon uses limited text and is neat and attractive. 1 2 3

Writing

3. What's the Story?

- The student adapts his or her newspaper article into a short story containing the same details. 1 2 3
- The story is entertaining rather than informative. 1 2 3
- The student uses descriptive language and action verbs to bring the story alive. 1 2 3
- The story is relatively free of errors in spelling, grammar, usage, and mechanics. 1 2 3

Crossing the Curriculum: Science

4. Tell Me Why

- The student chooses and researches an appropriate scientific question. 1 2 3
- The student writes an article that poses the question and then clearly and thoroughly explains the answer to the question. 1 2 3
- The article is relatively free of errors in spelling, grammar, usage, and mechanics. 1 2 3
- The student shares the article with the class or a school newspaper. 1 2 3

Chapter Three: *Choices* Activities

Evaluation Scale:	1 = Not at all	2 = To some extent	3 = Successfully

Crossing the Curriculum: Science

1. How Did That Happen?

- The student chooses and researches an appropriate scientific process.   1   2   3
- The student creates a flowchart or graphic that clearly shows the steps of the process.   1   2   3
- The flowchart or graphic illustrates each step and is neat and attractive.   1   2   3

Crossing the Curriculum: Speech

2. You Be the Teacher

- The student selects and learns how to make an appropriate product that will interest his or her audience.   1   2   3
- The student demonstrates to the class how to make the product.   1   2   3
- The student provides clear, precise directions and speaks audibly and clearly.   1   2   3
- The student provides neat and attractive visuals to help the audience understand the process.   1   2   3

Careers

3. Do You Have What It Takes?

- The student selects and researches an appropriate career.   1   2   3
- The student makes notes on the training, skills, and education required for the chosen career.   1   2   3
- The student writes a letter to a friend explaining how to enter the profession.   1   2   3
- The letter is relatively free of errors in grammar, spelling, usage, and mechanics.   1   2   3

Writing

4. Games People Play

- The student invents an appropriate, original game.   1   2   3
- The student writes clear and detailed instructions for playing the game, beginning by stating the goal of the game.   1   2   3
- The instructions list the steps required for playing the game in the correct order.   1   2   3
- The student provides a group of classmates with the instructions and materials needed to play the game.   1   2   3

Chapter Four: *Choices* Activities

> **Evaluation Scale:** 1 = Not at all 2 = To some extent 3 = Successfully

Careers

1. Tool Time

- The student chooses and researches an appropriate field.   1   2   3
- The student takes notes of examples of how people in the chosen career use comparing and contrasting in their work.   1   2   3
- The student writes a report that clearly and thoroughly describes specific examples of how people in the chosen career make comparisons.   1   2   3
- The report is relatively free of errors in spelling, usage, grammar, and mechanics.   1   2   3

Crossing the Curriculum: Art

2. An Eye for Detail

- The student creates two pictures in which several details have been changed from one to another.   1   2   3
- Each drawing contains recognizable details.   1   2   3
- The drawings are neat and attractive.   1   2   3
- The student shares the drawings with a partner who circles the items that are different.   1   2   3

Creative Writing

3. It's Like This

- The student uses an apt simile as the basis of the poem.   1   2   3
- The student explains the simile in a humorous way.   1   2   3
- The poem is arranged in lines rather than written as prose.   1   2   3
- The poem generally follows the conventions of grammar, usage, punctuation, and spelling except when conventions are not followed to create an effect.   1   2   3

Crossing the Curriculum: Music

4. The Beat Goes On

- The student chooses an appropriate band or musician and researches how the performer's music has changed or remained the same over time.   1   2   3
- The student makes notes focusing on differences or similarities in the performer's lyrics, musical style, vocals, or another area.   1   2   3
- The student gives a multimedia presentation that includes audio- or videotape segments illustrating the similarities or differences.   1   2   3
- The student speaks clearly and audibly during the presentation, and audio- or videotape segments are cued up and played at an appropriate volume.   1   2   3

Chapter Five: *Choices* Activities

▶ **Evaluation Scale:**   1 = Not at all   2 = To some extent   3 = Successfully

Careers

1. Everybody's a Critic

- With a partner, the student chooses an appropriate book or movie to review.   1   2   3
- The student reads the book or watches the movie and makes notes about why he or she likes or dislikes it.   1   2   3
- The student explains his or her opinion in a television review show format and supports the opinion using information from viewing notes.   1   2   3
- In a polite manner, the student discusses with a partner the points on which they agree and disagree about the book or movie.   1   2   3

Writing

2. That's What I Think

- The student chooses an appropriate novel to discuss with a pen pal.   1   2   3
- In a letter or e-mail, the student discusses the main character, setting, and plot.   1   2   3
- The student explains his or her reactions to the novel in the letter or e-mail.   1   2   3
- The student responds to the pen pal's comments about a novel the pen pal has read.   1   2   3
- The student writes at least two letters or e-mails.   1   2   3

Connecting Cultures

3. It's a Small World

- The student finds and reads at least two versions of the same story from different cultures.   1   2   3
- The student notes similarities and differences between the different versions of the story.   1   2   3
- The student creates a chart comparing the stories' characters, settings, and plot events.   1   2   3
- The chart is neat and attractive.   1   2   3

Technology

4. Virtual Critic

- In a group, the student helps develop criteria for evaluating educational computer games.   1   2   3
- The student helps create forms for evaluating the games.   1   2   3
- The student chooses an educational computer game, plays it, and completes the evaluation form.   1   2   3
- The student helps create a database record for each game, listing its evaluations based on each of the criteria.   1   2   3

Chapter Five: *Choices* Activities *(continued)*

Evaluation Scale:	1 = Not at all	2 = To some extent	3 = Successfully

Creative Writing

5. All Together Now

- The student writes a paragraph to contribute to a collaborative short story.   1   2   3
- The student actively participates in a revision discussion of the story and in a discussion of the experience of writing a story as a group.   1   2   3
- The student helps revise the story.   1   2   3
- The story is relatively free of errors in spelling, grammar, usage, and mechanics.   1   2   3
- The student helps the group orally present the final story to the class.   1   2   3

RUBRICS

Chapter Six: *Choices* Activities

▶ **Evaluation Scale:**	1 = Not at all	2 = To some extent	3 = Successfully

Careers

1. Expert Guidance

- The student chooses an appropriate career and arranges an interview to research the career. 1 2 3
- The student conducts an interview and takes notes about the education and training needed to enter the chosen field. 1 2 3
- The student writes a clear and accurate career guide entry based on notes from the interview. 1 2 3
- The writing generally follows the conventions of grammar, usage, punctuation, and spelling. 1 2 3
- The student works with classmates to create a neat and useful career guide including entries about a variety of fields. 1 2 3

Listening

2. My Kind of Tune

- The student researches the important elements of a particular style of music. 1 2 3
- The student chooses a recording of an appropriate example of the type of music researched. 1 2 3
- The student writes a review that evaluates how well the recording uses the elements the student identified as important. 1 2 3
- The student explains the review in a multimedia presentation. 1 2 3
- The student speaks clearly and audibly and the music is cued up correctly and at an appropriate volume. 1 2 3

Crossing the Curriculum: Physical Education

3. Hall of Fame

- The student chooses and researches an appropriate athlete. 1 2 3
- The student creates a trading card that notes important information about the athlete in an easy-to-read format. 1 2 3
- The trading card includes a picture of the athlete. 1 2 3
- The card is neat and eyecatching. 1 2 3
- The text of the trading card generally follows the conventions of grammar, usage, punctuation, and spelling, though fragments may be used for effect. 1 2 3

Chapter Six: *Choices* Activities *(continued)*

Evaluation Scale:	1 = Not at all	2 = To some extent	3 = Successfully

Creative Writing

4. A Fresh Angle

- The student uses one of the forms listed to clearly and thoroughly explain information learned through research.   1   2   3
- If the student writes a letter, it is entertaining and addresses the interests of a specific audience.   1   2   3
- If the student writes a short story, the research information is smoothly incorporated into the narrative.   1   2   3
- If the student writes a poem, the information is explained in a creative way, and ideas are arranged in lines rather than written as prose.   1   2   3
- The student shares the written product with others in one of the ways listed.   1   2   3
- The written product generally follows the conventions of grammar, usage, punctuation, and spelling except when conventions are not used to create an effect.   1   2   3

Chapter Seven: *Choices* Activities

▶ **Evaluation Scale:**	1 = Not at all	2 = To some extent	3 = Successfully

Editorial Cartoons

1. The Politics of Art

- The student chooses an appropriate editorial cartoon to analyze.   1   2   3
- The student creates a bulletin-board display that includes the cartoon   1   2   3
  and a one-paragraph analysis.
- The paragraph explains what the artist is trying to convince viewers   1   2   3
  to believe.
- The paragraph analyzes how the cartoon makes the persuasive point.   1   2   3
- The paragraph explains why the student was or was not persuaded by   1   2   3
  the cartoon.
- The paragraph generally follows the conventions of grammar, usage,   1   2   3
  punctuation, and spelling.

Careers

2. Persuasion in Practice

- The student chooses and researches an appropriate career.   1   2   3
- The student takes notes on how people in the chosen career field   1   2   3
  persuade others and what types of appeals they use.
- The student writes a short essay that clearly summarizes the information   1   2   3
  learned through research.
- The essay generally follows the conventions of grammar, usage, punc-   1   2   3
  tuation, and spelling.

Crossing the Curriculum: Social Studies

3. On the Go

- The student works appropriately with a small group.   1   2   3
- The group creates a petition consisting of a short letter and a form.   1   2   3
- The letter clearly identifies the proposed field-trip destination and pro-   1   2   3
  vides specific educational reasons for taking the class there.
- The form is neat and easy to read and provides spaces for student sig-   1   2   3
  natures and grade levels.
- The petition generally follows the conventions of grammar, usage, punc-   1   2   3
  tuation, and spelling, though fragments may be used for effect.

Chapter Seven: *Choices* Activities *(continued)*

Evaluation Scale:	1 = Not at all	2 = To some extent	3 = Successfully

Speaking

4. Talk Them into It

- The student chooses an appropriate issue for a persuasive speech.   1   2   3
- The student clearly states his or her opinion on the issue and makes a specific call to action.   1   2   3
- The student supports the opinion with reasons and evidence.   1   2   3
- The student organizes ideas in a logical way.   1   2   3
- The student speaks clearly and audibly and maintains audience interest.   1   2   3